THE PSYCHOLOGY OF HABIT ACCORDING TO
WILLIAM OCKHAM

THE PSYCHOLOGY OF HABIT ACCORDING TO WILLIAM OCKHAM

BY

OSWALD FUCHS, O.F.M. PH.D.

WIPF & STOCK · Eugene, Oregon

Wipf and Stock Publishers
199 W 8th Ave, Suite 3
Eugene, OR 97401

The Psychology of Habit According to William Ockham
By Fuchs, Oswald
ISBN 13: 978-1-4982-9488-1
Publication date 4/18/2016
Previously published by The Franciscan Institute, 1952

To The Queen of The Franciscan Order

ACKNOWLEDGEMENTS

The present publication is the doctoral diessertation presented by the author to the Faculty of the Franciscan Institute of St. Bonaventure University, St. Bonaventure, N.Y., U.S.A. Special acknowledgement and thanks are due to Rev. Philotheus Boehner, O.F.M., Ph.D., director of the Institute, under whose guidance this study was completed. Rev. Allan Wolter, O.F.M., Ph.D. and Rev. Eligius Buytaert, O.F.M., Ph.D. read the dissertion and made valuable suggestions. Thanks are due to the administration and the library staff of the University, particularly to Rev. Juvenal Lalor, O.F.M., Ph.D., President.

The author is also grateful to his religious superiors who gave him the opportunity for higher studies in the four universities from which he has received degrees: B.A. (Laval, Quebec), B. Ed. (Alberta), M.A. (Catholic University of America, Washington, D.C.), and Ph.D. (St. Bonaventure University).

A special debt of gratitude is owed to Most Rev. John Capistran Cayer, O.F.M., now Vicar Apostolic of Egypt; Rt. Rev. Damase Laberge, O.F.M., now Prefect Apostolic in Peru; Very Rev. Herve Blais, O.F.M.; Very Rev. George Albert Laplante, O.F.M.; Very Rev. Alphonse C. LaBoissiere, O.F.M. Finally, the author is indebted to his parents, relatives, and friends who by their encouragement and financial assistance helped in the realization of this project.

Table of Contents

INTRODUCTION

The facts concerning habit are a commonplace of our every-day existence. All our ordinary actions, like walking, eating, speaking, and the others, are attributable, in part at least, to acquired habits. Our social conventions and our moral behaviour reveal the effect of habits. Success in business, art and the professions is due in great measure to this same force.

These observable facts leave little room for discussion. The problem of habit is not whether there is such a thing, but rather how to explain it. What is the basis of habit, that is the question.

When modern Psychology discarded the philosophical systems of the Middle Ages, it considered the theory of habit as worth salvaging. In fact this factor seemed to lend itself readily to a physiological explanation of learning. Habit was given a physiological interpretation, and thus it seemed that a formula had been found which was satisfactory to both those who held that all learning consisted in habit-formation and to those who wished to reduce learning to nerve reactions.

In the present state of research, however, modern Psychology is obliged to abandon the identification of learning either with habit-formation or with the concomitant physiological phenomena. But the fault does not lie with the habit-theory itself. The root of the evil is to be found in the misguided attempt of physiologists to explain the higher processes in man by the lower, the spirit by matter. As long as the higher processes of man, as well as the lower, were viewed as innate powers, representing qualitatively, and not merely quantitatively, distinct abilities, developed through reaction with the environment, there was a place for habit. Thus the axiom, "practice makes perfect," had formerly a definite meaning, because it referred to the horizontal development of these abilities through exercise.

But when learning came to be considered as nothing more than the increasingly more complex mode of adjustment of man to the environment, then habit could no longer fit into the picture.

The emphasis being placed now on the ever-changing external stimuli as the cause of development, it appears difficult to see how the *learning* response resembles the *learned* response sufficiently to warrant the label of habit-formation in its traditional acceptation. Learning is represented as too fluid a process to warrant retention of habit as an explanatory factor. Virtually, therefore, if not admittedly, habit is an empty word in modern Psychology. The attempts of some Catholic scientists of the Experimental School to integrate the "neural pathways" explanation of habit into the traditional dualistic system of Catholic Psychology were rather an effort at compromise than an original contribution to psychology.

The theory of habit in empirical psychology received its first systematic, though perhaps somewhat incoherent, treatment at the hands of Aristotle. Later it was revived and amplified by the Scholastics of the late thirteenth century, and it seems to have reached the height of its development in the writings of William Ockham (+1349).

Neo-Scholastics have, it would seem, taken habit very much for granted. Its function in their systems is too important to permit of any challenge, and yet not important enough to deserve much new thinking apparently. The theories of the Medieval masters have been adhered to faithfully by textbook writers. However, even of these theories extensive studies were lacking until quite recently. At present there are, among others, two pieces of research worth mentioning: one by Vernon Bourke on habit according to St. Thomas, and the other by M. A. Rooney on habit according to St. Thomas and Godfrey of Fontaines (—1303). These are two doctoral dissertations, as yet unpublished, written at the Universities of Toronto and Montreal, respectively. To this list the present writer wishes to add the fruit of his labours, a study of Ockham's habit-theory.

What effect on the future of habit the combined impact of the opposing attitudes concerning it will have is not easy to foretell. The hope can be maintained, however, that in the hallways of the new emerging philosophies of the spirit a place will once more be found for habit, a philosophical entity as old as philosophy itself. In view of this, a better acquaintance with the theories of Medieval writers can serve a useful purpose. Of the predecessors of Ockham in the study of habit only brief sketches, unfortunately, can be given here. The list of these, which is not meant to be exhaustive, includes Aristotle, St. Thomas of Aquin, Godfrey of Fontaines, and Duns Scotus (+1308). The pattern, admittedly a bit artificial, into which the teachings of these philosophers on habit will be fitted consists in listing their definitions of the role of habit in each of the following processes: intellection and volition, sense cognition and sense conation. For Ockham's own teachings, which are the object of this study, it will be possible to create a setting which is closer to being a natural one. As the title indicates, our study is restricted to the philosophic concept of habit, and is exclusive of all theological implications.

ARISTOTLE

Aristotle's principles concerning habit, at least as known to the Scholastics, did not seem to lend themselves easily to a consistent interpretation. Our task is not to palliate these inconsistencies but to present the thought of the different passages where the Greek philosopher discusses habit, without reference to any particular interpretation.

The *Nicomachean Ethics* deal with habits as virtues, which are divided by Aristotle into intellectual and moral virtues. It is on the basis of praise or blame that a habit is considered moral and that some intellectual habits are called virtues.[1] Whether non-intellectual moral virtues are to be placed in the will or in the sense appetite according to Aristotle seems to have caused some difficulty. The answer seems to hinge on one's interpretation of the terms *irrational* in the Ethics, since it is said that these virtues reside in the irrational parts.[2] There is a text which seems to indicate that justice, at least, should be placed in the will, since it is defined as the virtue which makes man act justly and wish for what is just.[3]

The *Physics* represents moral and intellective habits, as well as physical conditions, to be the results of definite relationships

---

[1] Nic. Eth. 1, 13, 1103a, 9. Cf., *The Basic Works of Aristotle*: (R. McKeon) Random House, New York, 1941—*Ed.* I. Bekker, (*Opera Omnia*) Berlin, 1831 - 1870.

[2] *Ibid.* III, 9, 1117b, 23.

[3] *Ibid.* V, 1, 1129a, 9.

caused by alterations of the sensitive part of man's constitution; these alterations are produced by sensible objects.[4]

In Aristotle's *On The Soul* knowledge, in its habitual form, is said to be acquired by a change of quality, that is, by repeated transitions from one state to its opposite.[5] Knowledge in the actual state does not, however, constitute an additional change of quality. It represents the development of an existent quality from potentiality towards fixity (*habit*) or nature.[6] This development is dependent on the presence of the universals in the soul, as far as intellectual knowledge is concerned, and the presence of the sensible object, as far as sense cognition is concerned.[7] From this reference to universals in the soul have sprung the various theories on intelligible *species* among the Scholastics. Averroes, it seems, contributed to the conception of these *species* as active factors in intellection.[8]

In the *Metaphysics* Aristotle defines habit as a disposition by which a thing (or person) is well or ill disposed either in itself or with reference to something else. Health is given as an example of habit.[9] In the *Categories* habit is differentiated from disposition, which is described as less permanent and more changeable than the former.[10] Both however come under the classification of absolute qualities. On the other hand, it is noted at another place in the same book that, taken generically, habit can be considered as relative. Thus though we do not, explains Aristotle, talk about grammar of something, we do say knowledge of something.[11]

St. Thomas Aquinas

St. Thomas' study of habit is a fine example of his characteristic clarity and thoroughness. A brief sketch only of his teaching on this point is possible here. Habit is described by the Angelic Doctor as

---

4 Phys. VII, 3, 247a, 1-10.
5 On The Soul, II, 5, 417a, 32.
6 *Ibid.* 417b, 7.
7 *Ibid.* 417b, 23.
8 Averr. Comm. VI, De An. II, (Iuntas), 60.
9 Met. V, 20, 1022b, 12-14.
10 Cat. 8, 8b, 27.
11 *Ibid.* 7, 6b, 5. & Ib. 8, 11a, 20-32.

a quality[12] of the first species.[13] In the natural order a habit is said to inhere in a basic potency [14] and is by nature ordained to action.[15] It is considered as a necessary factor in the natural order of life, and the explanation of this necessity is deduced by St. Thomas from the nature of the principles of act and potency as applied to man. His faculties are in potency to several acts indeterminately, and to the same act in different manners.[16]

To explain habitual knowledge St. Thomas requires the actual presence of intelligible *species* in the intellect,[17] which are likenesses of the objects.[18] These *species* are the forms of material things abstracted from the phantasms,[19] and serve as *principia quo* of the knowledge of existing things.[20] Stored in the intellect, these same *species* are instrumental in the operations involved in retention and recall, at least in as far as universal concepts are concerned.[21] For retention and recall of knowledge of individual sensible things the intelligence must turn to the phantasms. In sense cognition St. Thomas also postulates *species* as media of knowledge.[22] These sensible species are called habits inasmuch as they dispose the sense cognitive powers to act in accordance with the dictates of reason.[23] which is also true of the dispositions favourable to virtue found in the sensitive appetite.[24] Concerning the *species* in the intellect it seems true to say that St. Thomas considers them habits inasmuch as they dispose the cognitive faculty to reproduce knowledge, acquired previously, at the command of the will, since he says expressly that habit from its very nature is principally related to the will, inasmuch it is that which one uses when one wills.[25]

12 Sum. Th. I-II, q. 49, a. 1.
13 *Ibid.* a. 2.
14 *Ibid.* q. 50, a. 2.
15 *Ibid.* q. 49, a. 3.
16 *Ibid.* a. 4.
17 Sum. Th. I, q.79, a.7, ad Ob. 3.
18 *Ibid.* I-II, q.50, a.5 ad 1.
19 *Ibid.* q. 85, a.1.
20 *Ibid.* a. 2.
21 *Ibid.* q. 79, a.7.
22 *Ibid.* q. 85, a.2.
23 Sum. Th. I-II, q.50, a.4.
24 *Ibid.* q. 56, a.4.
25 *Ibid.* q. 50, a.5.

Certainly the primary function of *species*, viewed as such, cannot
be other than to render possible knowledge of the objective reality
and its subsequent recall. This interpretation is further borne out
by St. Thomas' statements regarding the will as the real subject
of virtues viewed as moral habits. The other powers can be called
subjects of virtues only in as far as they are moved by the will.[26]

GODFREY OF FONTAINES

The study of Godfrey of Fontaine's Psychology throws considerable light on Ockham's teaching on habit. A short reference
to this author seems justified, therefore, in this introduction.

For Godfrey's concept of habit the writer will draw on the
above-mentioned dissertation of M. A. Rooney. First, with regard
to habit in the will, Godfrey seems to have relinquished an earlier
position and later opposed the traditional view that it exists in
the will. Moral virtues, according to his later opinion, exist as
habits primarily in the sensitive appetite.[27] This deviation is
attributable to the obscurity of Aristotle's text on this point in the
Ethics.

Concerning habit in the intellect, Godfrey is equally original
in his views. He denies the existence of *species* and views the act
of the intellect itself to be the likeness of the object. Habits required
to explain habitual knowledge are then easily accounted for. They
result from the repetition of acts, and are defined as dispositions
or impressions left in the potency, thanks to which it can reduce
itself to act more easily.[28] Godfrey admits habits in the internal
senses and sense organs.[29]

DUNS SCOTUS

Scotus accepts the intelligible *species*, and postulates habit as a
disposition distinct from the *species* in the intellect. The species can

---

[26] *Ibid.* q. 56, a.4.

[27] *Cf.* M. A. Rooney, *A Comparison of the Notions of Habitus in the
Philosophy of St. Thomas Aquinas and Godfrey of Fontaines*, Universite de
Montreal, Dissert. Unpubl. 1949, pp. 85-92.

[28] *Ibid.* p. 118.

[29] *Ibid.* p. 83.

indeed claim some of the characteristics of *habit* in that they dispose
the intellect to operate and are more or less permanent qualities
of this potency, yet they are not habits, properly so called. Habits
as such are abilities to reproduce past acts resulting from the
repetition of the original acts. They are not media of representation
or signification of the objects according to Scotus. This is the
peculiar function of the *species*.[30] As conserved in the intellect they
are instrumental in the processes of retention and recall of knowledge
acquired by this faculty.[31]

Moral virtues reside primarily in the will, according to the
Subtle Doctor.[32] They are produced by the virtuous acts of this
potency which has the power to choose the right form of behaviour.
As habits these virtues can exist in the will prior to the commands
it can give to the other faculties.[33] In the sense appetitive potency
habits can result as they continue to conform to the pattern of
behaviour imposed by the will. But these habits are not virtues
properly so called.[34]

Scotus further admits habits in the internal senses or imagination to explain the retention and recall of sense knowledge.[35] Physical
skills, as for instance those acquired by scribes and painters, are
explained by Scotus on the basis of habit-formation in the body.[36]

•   •   •   •

Against this roughly-sketched background the writer wishes
to present Ockham's theory of habit. This is not meant to be a
comparative study in the strict sense, and our reference to the
broader application of this theory in Ockham's system is no
reflection on the value of his predecessors' contributions. Furthermore, the question of the dependence of the Venerable Inceptor, as
Ockham was called, on his predecessors with regard to this theory

---

[30] Oxon. I, d. 3, q.6, n.29, (Vives) IX, 293a.
[31] *Ibid.* n. 27, IX, 291b.
[32] Oxon. III, d. 33, q. Un. n.2, XV, 438b.
[33] *Ibid.* n. 12, XV, 447b.
[34] *Ibid.*
[35] Oxon. IV, d. 45, q. 3, n. 19, XX, 350a.
[36] Oxon. III, d. 33, q. Un. n.19. XV, 455a.

is also beyond the scope of this study. Our aim is to make known a small but important segment of this fourteenth-century Scholastic's system. The method will be purely expository and not argumentative. With regard to the scope of our investigation, habit is the central theme but not as an isolated factor. It is viewed as an integrated element in a complex whole. Perhaps all that is needed to counteract the disrepute habit has fallen into in many circles is to present it in its proper systematic setting. Great disservice to habit was rendered by some pre-modern psychologists who ascribed to it a role for which it was not made. The discovery of its ineptitude caused its complete rejection by many. Therefore, it is obligatory in this investigation to introduce all the factors necessary for the appraisal of the exact position and role of habit.

Our study is divided into four chapters. The first presents the general principles governing habit-formation according to Ockham. In the second we see his application of this theory in the realm of cognitive experiences. The third examines its role in the conative reactions. In the fourth and last the moral implications of the habit-theory in human behaviour are reviewed.

The research work connected with this study involved first the ascertaining of the most reliable sources for Ockham's thinking. A trustworthy guide to his authentic works and the approximate dates of their composition has been prepared by Philotheus Boehner.[37] Apart from a few unrelated sections, edited by this same writer, Ockham's works do not exist in a critical edition. Our task it was therefore first to prepare a reliable text of the writings of Ockham pertinent to this topic. Old editions were used and corrected when necessary on the basis of the best known manuscripts, which were available to us in photostat form through the facilities of the Franciscan Institute, St. Bonaventure, N.Y.

---

[37] Philotheus Boehner, *The Tractatus de Successivis*, St. Bonaventure, N.Y., 1944, pp. 16-24. (Cf. *Ibid.* pp. 1-16 for biographical note on Ockham); Cf. *Traditio*, I, 1943, pp. 240-245; *The New Scholasticism*, XVI, 3, pp. 204-224.

SOURCES AND ABBREVIATIONS

Ordinatio Ockham (Commentarius in 1um Librum Sententiarum), (abbrev. *Ord.*) Old Edition: Lyons, 1495.[38] Recent Partial Edition: *Quaestio* 1^ *Prologi*, by Philotheus Boehner, Schoeningh, Paderborn, 1940; *Quaestio* 8^ Dist. 2^^E, The New Scholasticism, XVI, 3, 1942. pp. 224-241.

Reportatio Ockham (Quaestiones In 2^M, 3^M, et 4^M Libros Sententiarium) (abbrev. *Rep.*) Manuscripts: *Ob* Oxford Balliol, Coll. 299; *F* Firenze, Bibl. Naz. Conv. soppr. A. 3, 801.; *Ma* Paris, Bibl. Mazar. 893, s. XIV. Old Edition: Lyons, 1495.[38] Recent Edition: Rep. II, 14-15, by Philotheus Boehner, Traditio, I, 1943, pp. 245-275.

Quaestiones Variae (abbrev. *Rep. Quaest. Var.*) included in Lyons Edition, 1495,[38] (III, 12-15).

Quodlibeta VII (abbrev. *Quodl.*) Editions: Paris, 1487; Strasbourg, 1491 (references to this edition). Manuscript: Vat. Lat. 3075.

Summa Totius Logicae, Edition: Venice, 1508.

Summulae in Libros Physicorum (Philosophia Naturalis), Edition: Venice, 1506.

---

[38] Bound in one volume, original contemporary binding. (Franciscan Institute, St. Bonaventure, N.Y.)

CHAPTER I

GENERAL NOTIONS ON HABIT

1. DEFINITION AND CRITERION OF HABIT

For Ockham habit is a matter of experience, at least indirectly. It is said to exist when observation reveals the presence of certain specific elements of experience. These elements also constitute the basis of the Ockhamistic definition of habit. Thus when a person recognizes in himself, as a result of repeated acts, an acquired ability to do things or a certain facility of action which did not exist before, he can be said to possess a habit. By way of illustration, Ockham points to scribes, weavers and other artisans who gain proficiency in their tasks through the repetition of certain actions. To account for this acquisition, some force supplementary to the innate abilities of man must be postulated. That this power cannot be a negative but must be a positive factor is apparent from observation since there is no indication that anything had been forfeited in the process of acquisition. It is viewed, therefore, as a positive factor and included in the definition of habit, namely, an acquired ability to do certain things not possessed before or the ability to do them with greater ease or perfection than before.[1]

What was referred to as the criterion of the existence of habit and the elements of its empirical definition are said to exist not only in the realm of physical skills but also in that of mental operations. Experience shows that when a person has acquired knowledge or virtue he is capable of operations of which he was not capable before. This ability, which does not result from any deprivation in the intellect or the will, represents a positive acquisition. Knowledge and virtue, therefore, present the characteristics of habit. Many more examples would have to be cited to show the

---

[1] . . . potentia executiva corporalis per multos actus elicitos potest in consimiles actus in quos non potuit ante, vel saltem non ita faciliter ante tales actus, sicut patet in scriptoribus, textoribus, et in aliis artificibus. Ergo in illis potentiis est aliquid additum vel ablatum. Sed non apparet quod aliquid sit ablatum; ergo dicendum est quod aliquid sit additum. Illud voco habitum.— Quodl. (ed. Argent., 1491) III, 17.

1

full extent of the application of the habit-theory in Ockham. But that is not our purpose at this point. Our intention is only to indicate here that wherever it is applied the same basic criterion and definition is used.[2]

Ockham's empirical approach to the question of habit is clarified and corroborated by theological considerations. To the testimony of observation that habit represents a positive acquisition is added the testimony of Faith. Faith, he explains, teaches us that the intellective soul finds its ultimate happiness and perfection in heaven. To say that this state of bliss does not involve positive acts of the soul would, he claims, belittle considerably the eternal reward. If therefore acts may be viewed as positive entities, habits resulting therefrom may also be viewed thus and vice-versa. This inference stems from the traditional concept of causality according to which a positive effect requires a positive cause.[3]

In addition to the empirical and theological aspects of the question of the nature of habit there is also the ontological. This raises the issue of the place in the Aristotelian categories occupied by habit. Is habit a quality or merely a relationship? Aristotle's own views on the question are not easy to determine because of the contradictory statements to be found in his writings.[4] Ockham solved the problem in the light of his own metaphysical principles. According to his explanation of the ten categories, only two represent

---

[2] . . . omne quod potest in aliquam operationem in quam prius non potuit, nec est aliqua diversitas in passo, habet aliquam rem absolutam quam prius non habuit, vel caret aliqua re absoluta quam prius habuit. Sed habens illos habitus (*scientiam et virtutem*) potest in aliquam activitatem in quam prius non potuit intellectus vel voluntas; patet experientia. Nec est diversitas aliqua in passo, puta in intellectu vel voluntate.—*Ibid.* I, 18.

[3] . . . si actus est absolutus qui est generativus habitus, ergo et habitus erit. Quod autem actus sit absolutus probatur: quia per fidem nostram ultima operatio animae intellectualis est absoluta quia est nostra perfectio ultima, et si actus ille, igitur habitus generatus ex tali actu . . . Ponere enim quod beatitudo nostra et praemium nostrum nobis in coelo conferendum est tantum respectus est multum vilificare beatitudinem nostram.—Rep. (*ed.* Lyons, 1495, corr. with MSS F Ob.) III, 4, D.

Praeterea, actus elicitus est qualitas absoluta, ergo habitus. Consequentia patet, quia habitus est causa actus. Antecedens patet de felicitate nostra quam habemus per meritum quae est actus.—Quodl. I, 18.

[4] Aristotle's statements on the nature of habit are paraphrased in the INTRODUCTION, pp. xiii-xiv.

positive entities existing outside the mind, namely, substance and quality. The others are merely connotative terms. Therefore habit must be one of these two, since it is considered a positive factor. And as obviously it is not a substance, it must be a quality.[5]

Having proposed this solution, Ockham is faced with the necessity of interpreting the text of Aristotle's Physics[6] where the contrary view is proposed. First he reports Averroes' claim that the text in question did not represent the Stagirite's own thoughts but was a reproduction of those of Plato. Since this explanation did not seem very convincing to the Venerabilis Inceptor, he proposed his own. According to this, when Aristotle said habits are relationships, he was not formulating a general principle about all habits but was merely citing cases in which they can be considered as being only relationships. Such cases are given by Ockham. He gives the example of a person going to church with a bad intention. If this intention were changed into a good one while the action was still in progress, obviously the action would not have undergone any internal change. No real quality would have been added or taken away. The only alteration would consist in a changed relationship because of a change in the accompanying intention. In this instance the difference between a bad and a good action would consist in a changed relationship.

A similar example involving a knowledge-habit is given by Ockham. He supposes that he thinks someone present who is really not present. When this person later appears on the scene, the original judgment becomes true. Yet it will not change intrinsically since it reported the same fact in both cases. Here again, the difference between a true and a false proposition resides in the changed relation-

---

[5] Utrum virtus et scientia sint qualitates absolutae?

Ad quaestionem dico quod sic, quia omnes res est qualitas absoluta vel substantia. Sed virtus et scientia non sunt substantiae. Ergo sunt qualitates.— Quodl. I, 18.

. . . relatio non importat aliquem rem quae non sit de genere substantiae vel qualitatis, et tamen de nulla re praedicatur in quid; sicut simile non praedicatur in quid nec de homine nec de albedine, et hoc quia connotat plus quam illud de quo praedicatur, et sicut est de quantitate et relatione ita est de omnibus sex generibus aliis.—Expos. Aur. (ed. Bologna, 1496) Lib. Praed., XII, col. 4.

[6] Arist. Phys. VII, 3, 245b-248a (Cf. supra pp. xiii).

ship. But these are particular cases, Ockham would say. Any subjective change in the judgment entails a qualitative alteration.[7]

Habit is therefore a positive quality, belonging to an ontological system of thought. As such it is arrived at through reasoning, and cannot be an object of direct observation. It is known *a posteriori* from certain facts of experience which it is meant to explain. But these facts cannot be presumed to exist; their presence must be attested by observation. In this sense the existence of habit is contingent and dependent on empirical observation. Hence the empirical features of habit as described above.[8]

The contingent and empirical aspects of habit are further emphasized by the necessity of determining the conditions of its existence. First we shall examine the factors considered as causes of habit.

---

[7] Respondo uno modo sicut Commentator ibidem quod Aristoteles dicit hoc secundum opinionem Platonis et non secundum opinionem propriam.

Aliter tamen dico quod illud dictum est particulare et non universale, quia non intendit quod omnes formae de prima specie qualitatis sic sunt ad aliquid. Sed dicit tales particulares: scientia est ad aliquid; virtus est ad aliquid. Et tunc intendit dicere quod aliquis actus potest esse virtuosus qui prius non fuit virtuosus, et similiter accipiendo scire scil. large pro omni actu assentiendi. Aliter vero potest aliquis actus sine omni mutatione sui a parte esse actus sciendi qui prius non erat actus sciendi.

Exemplum primi: aliquis primo vadat ad ecclesiam propter vanam glcriam. Ista ambulatio est viciosus. Postea, stante eadem ambulatione, si mutet intentionem et velit ire propter Deum, tunc erit virtuosa, et tamen hic nulla est mutatio in actu ambulandi.

Exemplum secundi: quia ponatur quod assentiam huic propositioni: Sortes sedet; et opiner eam esse veram, quamvis ponamus quod sit falsa. Sed remanente intellectu in ipso assensu, videam Sortem sedere. Tunc modo scio istam propositionem, Sortes sedet, et prius non scivi eam; et tamen nulla mutatio est facta in illo actu assentiendi. Et sic intelligo Aristotelem in illo passu.—Quodl. I, 18.—Cf. Rep. III, 4, R. (*Cf.* Averrois Comment., Apud Juntas, Venetiis, VII, 20, F.P. 147 *Verso*).

[8] Notitia intuitiva, pro statu isto, non est respectu omnium intelligibilium, etiam equaliter praesentium intellectui quia est respectu actuum et non respectu habituum . . . sed potest tantum cognosci per rationem et discursum.—Ord. Prol. 1a. princ. XX, (ed. Boehner: p.48-49, 1-10).

II. HABIT-FORMATION

Habits are not inborn. This may be considered in a sense a foregone conclusion from the description of their nature, as given above, namely, powers accruing to a person under conditions dependent in a large measure on him. But Ockham gives additional proofs which are of interest because they serve to emphasize the distinction between habits on the one hand and instincts, appetites, and inclinations, which may be considered inborn on the other.

In arguing this point the Venerabilis Inceptor distinguishes three main types of habits: moral habits or virtues, intellective habits, and sense appetitive habits. He considers each separately.

First, moral habits or virtues are not inborn. Aristotle is referred to as the authority in this discussion.[9] He is quoted as saying that virtuous habits sometimes incline to acts contrary to nature. But something that is a part of our nature could not work against it.[10]

Ockham answers the objection made against this position by those who hold that Aristotle, while denying that habits were inborn in their developed state, maintained they were inborn inchoatively or in their roots (secundum inchoationem). The Venerabilis Inceptor refers to the Greek philosopher's own statement to the effect that habits are formed and increased by the same agent.[11] Thus, it is pointed out, if the origin of a habit could be attributed to nature, its complete development would also have to be attributable to nature. This everyone denies.[12]

---

[9] Nic. Eth. II, 1, 1103a, 19.

[10] Sed ista opinio est contra Philosophum, secundo Ethicorum, ubi probat quod virtus non est a natura, quia quando aliquis est assuetus ad contrarium illius ad quod natura inclinat, tunc illud non inest sibi a natura. Sed in multis acquirentibus virtutem est sic, igitur etc.—Rep. III, 11, C.

[11] Nic. Eth. II, 3, 1105a, 15.

[12] Si dicas quod Philosophus non intelligit quod virtus est a natura secundum suum esse completum sed secundum esse incompletum, quia secundum inchoationem ut praedictum est, contra. Philosophus probat quod ex eisdem generantur virtutes et augmentantur. Si igitur sint a natura secundum esse incompletum, igitur per consimiles actus possunt augmentari et esse a natura secundum esse completum, vel si non, tunc non augmentantur ex eisdem ex quibus generantur.—Rep. III, 11, C.

Secondly, in the cognitive faculties no habit is inborn, even inchoatively, because according to Aristotle the soul is at birth comparable to a clean slate *(tabula nuda)*.[13] This it would not be, says Ockham, if it had innate habits. Furthermore, he continues, the presence of habits at birth cannot be deduced from the fact that man can, without previous instruction, from the mere grasp of the notion of whole and part conclude that the whole is greater than the part. Even if all learning were forgotten, this proposition about the whole and the part would still appear true to the intellect. For additional evidence, Ockham refers to the Posterior Analytics,[14] where it is said that the knowledge-habits of first principles are acquired through experience and repeated act of knowing.[15]

Thirdly, there can be no question of inborn sense appetitive habits, even inchoatively, either in the soul or in the body. Indeed; man does at birth possess certain physical predispositions to virtue or vice, but these dispositions are not habits but physiological conditions similar to those conducive to health or ill-health. That these are not habits, Ockham explains, is demonstrated by the fact that they can be produced, increased, or diminished by artificial means, such as medical treatment. By such simple devices as, for example, stimulating the blood-circulation changes in these dispositions can be effected. Therefore they are not habits.[16]

Hence by whatever name the innate powers, urges, or inclinations of man are called, they do not reveal the characteristics of habit, one of which is that it is acquired as a result of man's own efforts.

---

[13] *Nic. Eth.* III, 4, 430a, 1.

[14] Post. Anal. II, 19, 100a, 9.

[15] Item de habitibus apprehensivis falsum est quia dicitur secundum Philosophum, tertio De Anima, intellectus est sicut tabula nuda in qua, etc. Sed si esset habitus principiorum secundum inchoationem, non esset sic, quia a natura haberet habitum licet secundum esse imperfectum. Item ratio sua est ad oppositum de habitu principiorum, quia destructo omni habitu, apprehensis terminis istis, totum et pars, statim sine omni habitu intellectus assentit. Item in secundo Posteriorum in fine probat Philosophus quod habitus principiorum acquiritur ex actibus sicut habitus scientiae, quia habitus principiorum acquiritur per multa experimenta.—Rep. III, 11, C.

[16] Item quod dicitur de appetitivis non videtur verum, quia illa dispositio corporalis non est habitus aliquo modo; sed est qualitas quaedam corporalis

Habits are acquired. Experience shows their existence to be linked with that of certain acts. It further reveals that this link is not merely one of temporal succession but of causality. Ockham uses the following empirical criterion to prove this. When two phenomena, he explains, appear together or in succession with such consistency that whenever one of them is posited the other invariably appears also, and whenever the former is not posited the latter does not appear, then it can be concluded that a causal link exists between the two. Habits function thus with regard to certain acts. It is a matter of daily experience that facility in the accomplishment of our tasks comes only as a result of efforts in performing them. Therefore habits can be said to be caused by acts.[17]

Habits exhibit a real causal relationship with acts, but this activity of the acts comes from a power that is relayed to them. They are themselves the products, at least in part, of the potencies of the substantial form.[18] Furthermore, in the very process of producing habits, acts need the co-operation of the potencies. Neither one nor the other can produce them alone.

---

vel multae qualitates praecedentes omnem actum, sicut qualitates proportionatae faciunt sanitatem.

Primum declaratur, quia non est magis inconveniens aliquid tale esse a natura ante omnem actum quam aliquod tale fiat vel augeatur per artem sine omni naturali actu. Sed per medicinam potest talis qualitas augeri vel minui, et potest aliquis per naturam et per medicinam inclinari ad actum intemperantiae, aliquis autem ad actum intemperantiae propter diversam complexionem naturalem. Patet de accensu sanguinis circa cor, quod ex aliis causis artificialibus causatur et minuitur.—Rep. III, 11, C.

[17] Quantum ad secundum articulum dico quod actus est causa efficiens respectu habitus, quod probatur: quia illud ad cuius esse ponitur aliud debet esse causa nisi evidenter appareat quod sit neganda causalitas. Sed posito actu frequenter elicito, ponitur habitus, et non potest poni naturaliter sine actu; et non apparet causa quare activitas debet negari ab actu. Ergo est causa effectiva actus.—Rep. III, 11, D.

[18] In Ockham's system the substantial form and its potencies can be referred to interchangeably as the source of activity, since they are not really distinct. Taking as illustration the example of the intellect and the will, he shows how these potencies or faculties are neither distinct from each other nor from the soul or substantial form. As a concept, *intellect* refers to the soul itself as capable of an intellective act; will represents the soul as capable of a volitive act.

Quarto dico quod . . . potentiae animae non distinguuntur ab anima nec

That acts be able to produce habits and then be themselves the effects of these habits may seem to involve an impossibility. And indeed it would if the same acts, numerically, were said to be both the causes and the effects of habits. But such is not the case. Those acts which cause habit and those which are caused by it are only specifically alike. not numerically identical.[19]

Acts are not only the causes of the genesis of habits but also of their development or strengthening. Modern experimental studies have been interested in showing the relation between the repetition of acts and the progressive development of habit. Although Ockham recognized the basic relationship, his empirical approach to the problem could not be expected to yield results comparable to those made possible by laboratory methods.[20]

Ockham's explanation of the development of habits is intimately connected with the traditional concept of causality. The criterion he applies is empirical and is based on the assumption that consistency of occurence implies causality.

III. ESSENTIAL EFFECT OF HABIT

The value of habit resides in its contribution to human proficiency. Basically, its contribution was described in Medieval terminology as an acquired ability to produce certain acts. Ockham posits a causal link between habits, on the one hand, and acts viewed as effects, on the other. In establishing this link, he applies the same

---

inter se . . . Intellectus et voluntas non differunt secundum istam viam nisi quia intellectus connotat actum intelligendi et voluntas connotat actum volendi; sed essentia animae non connotat aliquem actum.—Rep. IV, 2, K.

[19] Assumptum patet quia si activitas esset neganda ab actu, vel hoc esset . . . quia habitus potest totaliter causari a potentia, vel quia actus causatur ab habitu et non econverso propter certitudinem . . .

Nec secundum (*impedit*) quia si potentia est tota causa habitus, igitur potest causare habitum sine omni actu, quod falsum est, quia actus saltem primus potest causare sine omni habitu et non econverso. Nec tertium impedit quia in causis particularibus potest bene esse circulatio; et per consequens actus potest esse causa habitus, et ille habitus potest esse causa alterius actus et sic deinceps.—Rep. III, 11, D.

[20] . . . habitus generatus ex mille actibus circa principium excedit in intensione habitum generatum ex uno actu.—Ord. Prol. VIII, F.

empirical criterion as he used to explain the formation of habit, and credits Aristotle[21] with its authorship. It is said to be deducible from the Stagirite's definition of a cause: "causa est ad cuius esse sequitur aliud esse." It is to be noted, says Ockham, that this definition refers to an efficient and not a material cause. In the case of the habit-act relation the criterion is formulated in the following manner. Given a specific habit, certain acts can be posited in their partial or complete reality. If the habit is absent, these acts cannot exist either in their partial or complete reality. Habit, therefore, is truly the cause of acts.[22]

If habit is an ability to elicit acts, it can, in a broad sense, be termed a potency. But its features as a potency differ markedly from those of the potencies properly so called, namely, the intellect, will, etc. The latter are said to be potencies with reference to many acts indifferently: the intellect, for instance, to cognition involving truth or falsity; the will, to good or bad volitions. Habits, on the other hand, are determined to one type of act: good or bad, truthful or false. In this respect, habit is comparable to the object of a human act. It, too, is of itself limited to one mode of activity. It can act directly only on the potency by inclining it to act, whereas the potency receives both the object and the act.[23]

---

[21] Arist. Met. V, 2, 1013a, 25.

[22] Secundum Philosophum, quinto Metaphysicae, causa est ad cuius esse sequitur aliud esse; et loquitur de causa efficiente, non materiali, igitur etc. Tunc sic quando aliquid sic se habet ad aliud quod, ipso posito, potest aliud poni in esse simplici vel in esse perfecto; et ipso subtracto non potest poni in esse simplici vel in esse ita perfecto sicut cum isto, illud est causa huius. Sed posito habitu in potentia potest poni actus simpliciter tam in esse particulari quam in esse simpliciter; et isto subtracto, non potest poni simpliciter, tam in esse particulari quam in esse simpliciter nec in esse perfecto. Ergo habitus habet rationem causae respectu actus. Non autem habet rationem causae nisi efficientis, igitur etc.—Rep. III, 4, E.—Cf. Quodl. III, 18.

[23] Ideo dico quod potentia uno modo accipitur pro forma elicitiva multorum actuum indifferenter, et sic intellectus est potentia vel voluntas. Alio modo pro aliquo elicitivo unius actus determinate, et sic habitus potest dici potentia, et objectum similiter; unde potentia proprie est illimitata ad multos actus, sed habitus et objectum non. Similiter potentia recipit actum et objectum, habitus vero non.—Rep. III, 4, I.

Ad principale dico quod (*habitus*) non est potentia sicut auctores loquuntur de potentia, quia vocant potentiam illam quae potest elicere et recipere diversos actus et contrarios; et sic non est in potentia.—Quodl. III, 21.

Habit's immediate sphere of influence, as was said, is the potency or faculty itself. It inclines the faculty to act and shares in its activity. As a static element habit is viewed as an accidental form, adhering in the potency or in the form, since these are not distinct entities according to Ockham.[24]

As a more fundamental characteristic, it seems, potencies are differentiated from habits because they exist prior to all acts and are neither produced nor augmented by acts. Habits, however, depend on pre-existing acts for their existence, and on repeated acts for their growth and conservation.[25]

Habit's causal bearing on acts is of an auxiliary nature. It exercises an influence on the basic potency which is similar to that of the object. The coupled effects of the two on the potency can be cumulative, but that of habit is distinguishable from that of the object, and at times very easily. Indeed habit, when it is intense, is not only more potent than the object, but can be a decisive factor in the positing of certain acts which otherwise would not be posited. Taking the will as an example, the case can present itself where, in the presence of a certain object, it remains quite indifferent. If now in addition to these factors, kept constant, one were to postulate the presence of a deep-seated habit, then the inclination to act on the part of the will would be considerably enhanced. Indeed this inclination can be so great that resistance to it can become practically impossible. Ockham considers this as evidence of the effectiveness of habit.[26]

---

[24] Tamen habitus proprie inclinat potentiam, quia est forma perficiens potentiam, et cum hac ut causa partialis inclinans ad actum.—Rep. III, 4, M.

[25] . . . distinctio est quod potentia praecedit actum, nec augmentatur nec generatur per actum; habitus sequitur actum et generatur et augmentatur per actum.—Rep. IV, 2, D.

[26] Aliquando posita causa partiali, puta objecto, ponente potentia et deficiente habitu, non inclinatur potentia ad actum quia potest exire in actum et non exire sine aliqua difficultate, et ita faciliter exiret in actum in absentia objecti sicut in praesentia, loquendo maxime de actu qui est in potestate voluntatis. Sed existente habitu in potentia cum aliis requisitis vix potest homo resistere sine magna difficultate quando exeat in actum secundum inclinationem habitus qui eum quasi impellit ad hoc sicut cum experimur in nobis maximam repugnationem et difficultatem resistendo inclinationem habitus, igitur habet activitatem.—Rep. III, 4, E.

The preceding paragraphs may be summarized in a few statements. The causal link between habits and acts is a two-way link. The apparent contradiction in this statement is removed by the explanation that the acts involved are similar but not identical. The habit-theory is used to account for the observable fact that some acts have a residual effect on subsequent acts of a similar nature. Its operativeness is, however, not deduced *a priori* from the indeterminate nature of the potencies and their inability to evince fixed patterns of action. It is proven on the basis of observation.

IV. DIFFERENTIATION OF HABITS

The residual effect which some acts can have with regard to subsequent acts of the same nature—a fact which is expressed in the popular saying: practice makes perfect—presupposes a certain characteristic on the part of habit which is very important. The habit or trace caused by several acts of the same nature must be a single entity. In other words, the effects of these acts must be cumulative and be able to produce something that is organically one and simple. To have this effect, how much alike must acts which contribute towards it be? This is the question of the differentiation of habits.

The key to the solution of the problem is to be found in the very notion of specific unity. Acts, it is admitted, can be numerically different and yet have the one and same effect. It is in virtue of the likeness of these acts that they can have this effect. On the basis of their like or unlike natures, acts are said to be specifically the same or specifically different. For each specifically similar group of acts Ockham posits the possibility of a single effect by way of habit-formation. Habits are therefore differentiated on the basis of the acts which produce them.

The truth of this statement can, according to Ockham, be ascertained on the basis of experience. The repetition of certain acts yields facility in the performance of these same acts but not of any others. In other words, observation reveals that the practice of one skill or operation produces no notable effect on our ability in other skills or operations, at least if these are unrelated to the former.

Examples are given to illustrate the specific distinction of acts which yield different habits. Simple apprehension or *incomplex*

knowledge is specifically distinct from judgment or *complex* know
ledge. Similarly, knowledge of a premise is really and specifically
different from that of a conclusion. Now if these forms of cognition,
viewed for instance as habitual knowledge, are distinct it must be
because the acts which produced them are specifically different from
each other, for like causes produce like effects.[27]

Habits are distinguished, therefore, on the basis of acts. But
acts themselves are classified according to the nature of the objects
to which they have reference. Ultimately, therefore, the differentiation of habits is based on the accepted classification of objects.
Ockham sees no other possible criterion. Unless, says he, we admit
that there be distinct acts and habits for each specifically distinct
object, there is no means of deciding which acts or habits are specifically distinct from any others.[28]

Though specifically distinct objects cannot produce one individual act or habit, it does not follow that one object cannot be
cognized by different subjective acts or processes. Ockham gives the
example of intuitive and abstractive cognition, which can apprehend
the same object. Still the acts by which it is done are specifically distinct, and so would the resulting habits be, if there were any in
intuitive cognition. He draws an *a fortiori* argument from this for
the possible distinction of acts and habits in the case of distinct
objects.

---

[27] Et quantum ad primum intellectum (*modum intelligendi*) dico quod
tanta est distinctio actuum quanta est habituum, et econverso. Tum quia
distincti habitus specie sunt a distinctis actibus specie, quod non esset nisi
esset equalis distinctio eorum. Tum quia econverso distincti actus specie causant
distinctos habitus specie. Quod patet quia habitus generati ab istis actibus
non inclinant immediate nisi ad consimiles actus et non ad alios; et alius
habitus generatus ab aliis actibus inclinat ad alios actus, etc.

Praeterea, causae eiusdem rationis possunt causare effectus eiusdem
rationis. Sed habitus generatus ex actibus non possunt frequenter esse eiusdem
speciei, quod patet de habitu respectu complexi et incomplexi; et respectu
conclusionis et principii. Ergo nec actus possunt esse eiusdem speciei.—Quodl.
II, 18.—Cf. Ord. Prol. VIII, F; Rep. III, 11, J.

[28] Praeterea nisi distinctorum objectorum specie essent actus distincti et
habitus, non posset probari distinctio specifica inter quoscumque actus vel
habitus.—Quodl. II, 18.

Habits and acts related to one sort of objects are not only alike in one mind but also as compared to the minds of other humans. In making this remark, Ockham draws no particular conclusion, but its implications are obvious. Comparison and communication of thoughts would be impossible, if our reactions to individual objects would *a priori* be accepted as essentially different.[29]

The value of habit, as can be seen from these paragraphs, resides in the economy of energy it entails. One habit records many single experiences and permits of their recall. If one had to be continuously relearning the same things, no progress would be possible. But what of the relations between habits? Are they to be viewed as so many grooves or patterns of action which run parallel but never meet, or which stratify human reactions to the point of automatism? Experience shows that such is not the case. Habits as individual units fit into a broader framework where the same process of unification goes on but on a larger scale, where the same principle of economy prevails, and where the mind's dominion over matter becomes most manifest.

V. INTEGRATION OF HABITS

The process of unification or integration of elemental units or habits of learning was certainly present to Ockham's mind when he elaborated his doctrine of the universals. For him, *universalizing* was a process of the mind. It did not mean taking cognizance of would-be universals outside the mind. The world of realities is made up of singular things. On the basis of these singulars the mind constructs common or universal concepts. This is described by Ockham as a hidden process and a natural operation of the mind. The point of departure is known—it is the singular. The point of arrival is also known—it is the universal. But what process links these to each other remains a matter of speculation.[30]

---

[29] Praeterea, respectu eiusdem objecti numero possunt esse cognitiones alterius speciei. Patet de cognitione intuitiva et abstractiva. Ergo multo magis respectu objectorum distinctorum specie.

Et respectu eiusdem principii tam actus quam habitus in diversis intellectibus sunt eiusdem speciei.—Quodl. II, 18.

[30] Ad septimum dico quod natura occulte operatur in universalibus; non quod producat universalia extra animam tamquam aliqua realia, sed quia

Habit is not used by Ockham to explain the entire process of integration or universalization. But it is made to fit into this process. Before there can be habits in this system, there must be acts; before there can be integrative habits, there must be integrative acts. That there are such acts prior to habits proves that the process of integration is a natural function of the potencies. Examples of such acts are, according to Ockham, judgments where two terms are combined and where two or more propositions are grasped by one act. He sees no reason why the intellect should not be able to hold in consciousness both the premises and conclusions of a syllogism. Not only do such acts occur, but habits corresponding to them are formed. Since the function of these habits is to retain and, upon occasion, to reproduce such comprehensive concepts, it is clear that they facilitate further unification and integration. In this manner they fit into the integrative process of the mind.[31]

The acts reproduced by habits, it must be emphasized, are not different from those learned, that is, previously elicited. Thus a highly integrated act can form a habit and the immediate result of this habit will be that same integrated act. However, this act can bring in its train, as it were, all its unified elements, and in this manner the same habit can be said to be cause of several distinct, though related, acts. Taking the example of a syllogism grasped by one unified act, Ockham explains that the immediate result of the corresponding habit is the reproduction in the mind of the entire syllogism—premises and conclusions. Indirectly, this habit can call to mind such inferences which might have been drawn

---

producendo cognitionem suam in anima quasi occulte saltem immediate vel mediate producit illo modo quo nata sunt produci; et ideo omnis communitas isto modo est naturalis et a singularitate procedit. Nec oportet illud quod isto modo fit a natura esse extra animam sed potest esse in anima.—Ord. I, d.2, q.7, *CC*.

[31] Tertio dico quod principiorum aliquorum et conclusionum potest esse idem habitus. Hoc probatur: respectu quorumcumque est natus esse aliquis habitus respectu quorum est unus actus. Sed respectu praemissarum et conclusionum potest esse unus actus, quia non plus repugnat sillogismo composito ex multis propositionibus intelligi uno actu quam propositioni compositae ex multis terminis. Sed propositio intelligitur uno actu.

Ideo dico uniformiter de habitibus et actibus quod semper proportianter secundum identitatem et diversitatem, quia semper est tanta identitas et diversitas in habitibus quanta est in actibus, ex quibus generatur habitus vel augmentatur.—Ord. Prol. VIII, F.

from the conclusion of the syllogism before the habit was formed. With regard to the first conclusion habit would be the immediate cause, and with regard to subsequent conclusions the mediate or remote cause—causa causae.[32]

Against this background of habits in the integrative process of the mind, Ockham treats the question of the unity of science. If a science included only such elements as could be chained together logically, then this science could be called a single unit. But those sciences generally studied in his time did not reveal this internal cohesion. Thus Metaphysics, Natural Philosophy, and others, included not only syllogistic arguments but notions of terms, refutations of false arguments and of errors, and rectification of these errors, and so on. Obviously there was no link between all these disparate elements, that is, no logical link which permitted them to be grasped in one comprehensive act of the mind. Consequently no single habit could be expected to store knowledge of all these elments. At best, therefore, science could be considered as a collection or aggregation of habits.[33]

Theology, as a human science, reveals the same characteristics, according to Ockham. It includes elements of natural faith, evident propositions and inferences, and apprehensive acts of terms (*incomplexa*) and of propositions (*complexa*). In this sense it, too, is merely a collection of habits.

---

[32] Sciendum est tamen quod unus habitus potest inclinare ad actus distinctos specie, ita tamen quod ad unum actum inclinet immediate et ad aliud vel multos alios mediate, quia habitus principii inclinat immediate ad actum elicitum circa unam conclusionem, et mediante illo secundo potest habitus primus inclinare ad aliud actum circa eandem conclusionem; et sic de multis conclusionibus ordinatis. Et tunc primus habitus ad primum actum ordinatur sicut causa immediata ad effectum immediatum, et ad secundum et tertium actum et deinceps ordinatur sicut causa remota ad effectum remotum et est causa causae.—Rep. III, 11, K.

[33] Aliquando accipitur (*scientia*) pro collectione multorum habituum ordinem determintum et certum habentium. Et isto modo accipitur scientia frequenter a Philosopho. Et scientia isto modo comprehendit tamquam partes aliquonimodo integrales habitus principiorum et conclusionum, notitias terminorum, reprobationes falsorum argumentorum et errorum, et solutiones eorum; et sic dicitur Metaphysica esse scientia et Naturalis Philosophia esse scientia, et ita de aliis.—Expos. Sup. Oct. Lib. Phys., Prol. (ed. Mohan) p. 240. (Francis. Stud., 1945, V) Cf. Ordin. Prol. q. 1, H.

Viewed, however, as a supernatural gift of Faith, Theology manifests greater internal cohesion, and can be considered one single habit.[34]

The integrative powers of the human mind are not restricted to the speculative field where logic holds sway. They extend to the realm of practical knowledge and even to that of conative endeavour. In the field of practical knowledge, prudence is said to be the dominating factor. It dictates courses of action, but as an intellective process it can be resolved into syllogistic arguments. These permit of a comprehensive grasp in the same manner as the more speculative type. This grasp can result in a single comprehensive habit. This habit will call to mind, when the occasion presents itself, not only this comprehensive act, but the whole series of practical considerations one may have linked to it prior to the formation of the habit. These provide norms of behaviour in the everchanging circumstances of man's moral existence.

Integration, according to Ockham, is also present in the realm of conative experiences, although naturally it does not manifest the same psychological characteristics as in the intellect. Under the heading of connection of virtues this particular aspect of the general process received considerable attention from Ockham, as it had from his predecessors. We shall have to revert to it later[35] when we discuss the virtues in detail. But the fact of its existence may be recorded at this point. According to the Venerabilis Inceptor, virtues in the will are linked to the extent, at least, that the perfect possession of one entails a disposition or inclination to all others.[36]

---

[34] Alio modo Theologia includit fidem acquisitam et aliquos habitus evidentes tam propositionum quam consequentiarum et habitus apprehensivos omnium sive complexorum sive incomplexorum, et isto modo non est una numero . . .

Circa secundum principale dico quod Theologia uno modo includit fidem infusam. Et Theologia secundum istam partem est una unitate numerali, quia fides infusa est una numero.—Ord. Prol. VIII, G. 2-6.

[35] Chap. IV, p. 98.

[36] Ad aliud de unitate prudentiae dico proportionabiliter de unitate prudentiae sicut de unitate habitus ut in Prologo dictum est quod est alia prudentia habitualis et actualis principii et conclusionis; et quot sunt complexa distincta circa quae potest esse prudentia tot sunt habitus distincti et actus.

In the preceding pages a rapid sketch has been provided of Ockham's theory of habit. First it was noted that both the definition and the criterion of existence of habit rested on data of experience— an acquired ability to do things in a manner or with a degree of perfection unknown before. Next, the formation of habit was described with special emphasis on its dependence on acts. Then, habit's activity with regard to acts similar to those which produced it was described. Following that, we discussed the basis of the differentiation of individual habits, which we found to be none other than the specific nature of the acts themselves. Finally, habits role in the process of integration was outlined. Taking up the study of habit more in detail now, according to Ockham, we find it advisable to begin with its function in the cognitive processes.

Similiter unus potest esse habitus prudentiae mediante quo intelligitur et conclusio.—Ord. Prol. VIII, F.

Alio modo connectuntur (*virtutes*) inclinative et dispositive, sic quod qui habet unam virtutem perfecte habet inclinationem et principium partiale efficiens respectu omnium virtutum.—Rep. III, 11, X.

CHAPTER II

Habits In The Cognitive Processes

In Ockham's Psychology, as in all Medieval systems, one must distinguish two levels of cognition or two realms of awareness: the one, immaterial or spiritual, namely, the intellective; the other material or sensate, namely, sense cognition. According to the Venerabilis Inceptor, habit plays an important and characteristic role in each. For a better graps of his thought, it is advisable to begin with habit's function in intellective cognition.

I. On The Intellective Level

Intellective cognition comprises actual knowledge and recall of past experiences. Habit contributes to the production of both, according to Ockham. Actual knowledge, on the other hand, includes perception of reality, assertions or denials about reality, and lastly, inferences and argumentation. The perceptive function is performed by two distinct processes in Ockham's system: intuitive and abstractive cognition. Beginning with intuitive cognition, we shall give as complete a description of all the intellective processes indicated as is necessary for the understanding of the role of habit in each.

1. IN INTUITIVE PERCEPTION

Perception is the most fundamental and basic act of intellective cognition. The act by which the simplest unit of reality, called an *incomplexum,* is perceived is a simple apprehensive, or an *incomplex* act. The apprehensive act serves as basis of judgments about the perceived object. When the judgment bears on the actual existence or non-existence of the object, or on any other contingent truth concerning it, then it can be an evident judgment only if the reality described is such as reported at that moment. For this to be possible, the apprehensive act must be able to report such contingent facts. Ockham maintains that it can, and considers this act psychologically distinct from the one which does not report such facts. He terms it intuitive cognition. It furnishes the evidence for the judgment

18

about contingent occurrences, and the degree of evidence will depend on the perfection of the intuitive act.[1]

Though intuitive cognition reports the contingent circumstances of reality, which are true only at the time of the perceptive act, it is nevertheless basic to all experiential knowledge. Without it there would be no contact with the world of reality and no knowledge of those truths called necessary, because they are derived from our contact with reality.[2]

The object known by intuitive cognition must not be viewed, according to Ockham, as a composite reality, comprising an essence and an existence separately knowable. It is the total object as it exists in reality, that is, the singular individual, which presents itself to the perceiving intelligence. The distinction between what is contingent and what is not contingent in a particular situation is the result of the mind's operation rather than of the activity of the object with regard to the intellect. Each object is singular and, as such, unique. Being a natural cause, and not free, it can have only one effect, as far as it is concerned, on any perceiving faculty. It is evident therefore that Ockham maintains the intellect's ability to know the singular. Furthermore he denies that Aristotle held the intellect could know *only* the universal. According to the Venerabilis Inceptor, the Stagirite's[3] famous adage means that the senses know

---

[1] Et universaliter omnis notitia incomplexa termini vel terminorum, seu rei vel rerum, virtute cuius potest evidenter cognosci aliqua veritas contingens, maxime de praesenti, est notitia intuitiva . . .

Notitia intuitiva rei est talis notitia virtute cuius potest sciri utrum res sit vel non, ita quod si sit res statim intellectus judicat eam esse, et evidenter cognoscit eam esse, nisi forte impediatur propter imperfectionem illius notitiae.— Ord. Prol. I, Z.—Cf. Rep. II, 14-15, G.

[2] Et illa notitia est intuitiva a qua incipit experimentalis notitia, quia universaliter ille qui potest accipere de aliqua veritate contingenti experimentum, et mediante illa de veritate necessaria, habet aliquam notitiam incomplexam de aliquo termino, vel de re, quam non habet ille qui non potest sic experiri . . . Et tamen certum est quod illae veritates (*contingentes*) possunt evidenter cognosci, et omnis notitia complexa terminorum vel rerum significatarum ultimate reducitur ad notitiam incomplexam terminorum vel rerum significatarum. Ergo isti termini vel res una alia notitia possunt cognosci quam sit illa virtute cuius non possunt cognosci tales virtutes contingentes. Et ista erit intuitiva.—Ord. Prol. I, Z.

[3] On The Soul, II, 5, 417b, 23-30.

only the singular, while the intellect knows both the singular and the universal.[4]

The singular object is considered a cause of the intuitive perception, and therefore could not be known intuitively if it did not exist, except through special Divine intervention.[5] The object and the intuitive act are partial causes of the judgment concerning the existence of the object when it exists. When it does not exist, however, the object's causality is, naturally speaking, withdrawn. The judgment of non-existence which then results is produced with the collaboration of the perceptive act alone. Ockham thus explains how judgments about existence differ from those about non-existence. In the former, the effect of the object is added to that of the perceptive act, and in the latter it is not.[6]

Having determined the relationships which exist between the various forms of actual knowledge, we come to the study of habitual knowledge. That this type is also, in some manner, linked to our intuitive grasp of objective reality is attested by Ockham's references to Aristotle, where he says that "science and art come to men through experience,"[7] and "intuition will be the originative source of scientific knowledge."[8] The Venerabilis Inceptor adds that just as scientific

---

[4] Dico quod intellectus pro statu isto cognoscit singulare, et primo sicut alias patebit, et est primum cognitum primitate generationis.

Nec Aristoteles negat, sed ponit quod intellectus intelligit (*etiam*) universale, sensus autem cognoscit singulare.—Ord. Prol. I, TT. Cf. Quodl. I, 13. . . . idem totaliter et sub eadem ratione ex parte objecti est primum objectum sensus exterioris et intellectus primitate generationis.—Ord. Prol. I, TT.

[5] The question of the possibility of intuitive cognition of non-existents will not be gone into here. For an authoritative discussion on the problem the reader is referred to: Philotheus Boehner, *The Notitia Intuitiva of Non-existents according to William Ockham* (Traditio, New York, V, 1943, No. 1) pp. 223-240.

[6] Et ideo notitia intuitiva rei propria et res causant iudicium quod res est quando est. Quando autem ipsa res non est tunc notitia intuitiva sine illa re causabit oppositum iudicium. Et ideo concedo quod non est eadem causa illorum iudicium, quia unius causa est notitia sine re, alterius causa est notitia cum re, tamquam cum causa partiali.—Ord. Prol. I, ZZ.—Cf. *Ib.* HH.

Ideo dico quod notitia intuitiva et abstractiva seipsis differunt et non penes objecta . . . quamvis naturaliter notitia non possit esse sine existentia rei, quae est vere causa efficiens notitiae intuitivae mediata vel immediata.— *Ib.* G.G.

[7] Met. I. 981a, 2.

[8] Post. Anal. II, 7, 100b, 15.

knowledge dealing with sensible things originates with the intuitive cognition, by the senses, of these things, so the scientific knowledge of purely immaterial things must originate with the intuitive grasp by the intellect. And one need hardly explain that scientific knowledge involves habitual knowledge, especially since it is not excluded by Ockham when he says: " . . . universaliter notitia scientifica . . . incipit a notitia instutiva." Since the very notion of habitual knowledge, at least in Medieval thinking, implies habits,[9] we are faced with the problem of the relation between intuitive cognition and habit-formation.[10]

The question is: can intuitive cognition produce habits? Above all, can it produce habits or habitual knowledge of abstractive knowledge? In solving this problem, Ockham was obviously caught on the horns of a dilemma. To say that intuitive cognition could cause habits of abstractive knowledge would be a simple solution and in accord with certain data of experience, which does not indicate the presence of any intermediary factor between intuitive perception and the formation of habits of abstractive knowledge.[11] On the other hand, this explanation would destroy the mechanics of the habit-theory, according to which habits and the acts linked with them causally are always of the same nature. But knowledge of facts as existing or not existing is different specifically from knowledge of facts without regard to existence or non-existence. Furthermore habits, specifically intuitive, do not seem to be warranted by observation. Even after repeated intuitive acts, they are not facilitated to the point of not requiring the presence of the object. Therefore, no habit-forming can be justified on that score.

---

[9] Though the word *habitus* is commonly used by Scholastics, some of the explanations of habitual knowledge, as for instance the species-theory, differ greatly from Ockham's. This difference will become increasingly clear as we proceed.

[10] Et ideo sicut secundum Philosophum, primo Metaphysicae et secundo Posteriorum, scientia illorum sensibilium quae accipitur per experientiam de qua ipse loquitur, incipit a sensu et a notitia intuitiva sensitiva istorum sensibilium.

Ita universaliter notitia scientifica istorum pure intelligibilium accepta per experientiam incipit a notitia intuitiva illorum intelligibilium.—Ord. Prol. I, Z.

[11] Because Ockham's text introduces the notion of abstractive cognition which we will explain later we prefer not to quote it here. The reader may refer to it on page 25, n. 20.

To adopt the first view meant to reject the habit-theory. That Ockham did not do that is proof at once of the importance of the theory to his mind and of greater conservatism than many historians are willing to attribute to him.[12] The position that intuitive cognition produces no habits was held consistently throughout his works.[13]

To substantiate the thesis that intuitive cognition is the originative source of all scientific knowledge, including habitual knowledge, an intermediary factor must be postulated between the former and the latter. It must be something that can produce cognitive habits and be itself linked with the intuitive act. Thus, the exigencies of the habit-theory are satisfied and the dependence of habitual knowelge on perception of objective reality is maintained. What this factor is and how it performs this role will be discussed in the following section.

2. IN ABSTRACTIVE COGNITION

Science or scientific knowledge, either actual or habitual, is in Ockham's epistemological system synonymous with non-existential knowledge. And by non-existential is meant that which abstracts from the *hic et nunc* existence or non-existence of things, as well as the *hic et nunc* inherence in a subject of accidental qualities, etc. As was seen above, he considered the process by which these circumstances are perceived distinct from the one whereby the object was known as divested, so to speak, of these elements. The former he called intuitive cognition, and the latter was called abstractive cognition.[14]

---

[12] Hochstetter thought there was evidence to show that Ockham favoured the first theory because he thought it was implied in subsequent writings. Cf. *E. Hochstetter, Studien zur Met. und Erkenntnisl. W. von Ock.* (Berlin, 1927), p. 70ff. This has been disproved, however, by Philotheus Boehner, op. cit. p. 227.

[13] Si dicis quod ex cognitione intuitiva perfecta frequenter elicita potest generari habitus, respondeo quod ex nulla cognitione intuitiva sensitiva vel intellectiva potest generari habitus . . . quia nullus experitur quod magis inclinatur ad cognitionem intuitivam post talem cognitionem frequenter habitam quam ante omnem cognitionem intuitivam, quia sicut prima cognitio intuitiva non potest naturaliter causari sine existentia objecti et praesentia, ita nec quaecumque alia nec plus inclinatur ex tali cognitione frequenti quam in principio.—Rep. 14-15, H.

[14] Ad septimum dico quod intellectus non semper abstrahit ab hic et nunc

Abstractive knowledge, as a psychological phenomenon, is recognizable therefore as that type of cognition which makes things known to us as objects of knowledge but does not permit us to assert that they exist or do not exist. Thus I can know Socrates and know the colour *white* and yet be unable to say whether Socrates is white, or not white, whether he is here or there, and so on for all the other contingent circumstances. This is abstractive cognition. As viewed here, abstractive cognition is an *incomplex* form of knowledge and can serve as a basis for judgments in a manner similar to the intuitive. The nature of the judgment is, of course, dependent on the kind of *incomplex* cognition from which it derives its evidence.[15]

This notion of abstraction, as implied in abstractive cognition, does not presuppose the composition of essence and existence on the part of the object, nor the separability in it of essence and material conditions. It does not mean that by abstractive cognition the intellect can view one of these would-be objective elements independently of the others. As was said when we discussed intuitive cognition, Ockham considers the object of intellective cognition in itself to be in no manner different from the object of sense cognition. Of course, only material objects can be perceived by the senses, but these can also be perceived directly by the intellect in the present state ("pro statu isto"). Thus the object of intellection which is first in the order of generation of knowledge is no more an abstract entity than the object of the senses.[16]

in omni intellectione, quamvis in aliqua sic abstrahit quia sicut intellectus habet notitiam per quam iudicare non potest de hic et nunc, hoc est, quod res sit hic et nunc . . . et illa est notitia abstractiva . . . Ord. Prol. I, TT.

[15] Similiter per notitiam abstractivam nulla veritas contingens, maxime de praesenti, potest evidenter cognosci; sicut de facto patet quod quando cognoscitur Sortes et albedo sua in absentia virtute illius incomplexae notitiae non potest sciri quod Sortes est vel non est, quod est albus vel non albus, vel quod distat realiter a tali loco vel non, et sic de aliis veritatibus contingentibus. —Ord. Prol. I, Z.—Cf. II, 14-15, Z; *Ib.* 16, JJ.

[16] Si dicitur quod intellectus abstrahit a materia et a conditionibus materialibus, dico quod illa abstractio non est intelligenda ex parte objecti in omni intellectione; quia dico . . . quod idem totaliter et sub eadem ratione ex parte objecti est primum objectum sensus exterioris et intellectus primitate generationis, et hoc pro statu isto. Et ita objectum intellectus in illa prima intellectione non est magis abstractum quam objectum sensus.—Ord. Prol. I, TT.

After it has performed the initial act of perception of the singular object, the intellect can abstract and isolate certain concepts which are common to many. It can consider these in an object and exclude others. The senses do not share this prerogative. Thus abstraction is a process of the mind. It is an immaterial process, which the senses cannot share.[17]

Though abstractive cognition is viewed by Ockham as derived from the real, singular, existing object, its contact with this object is not immediate. It presupposes in every case an act of intuitive cognition.[18]

This dependence of abstractive cognition on intuitive can be interpreted in two ways. It can mean that it depends on intuitive cognition as habitual knowledge and that no habit of abstractive knowledge can be formed until the object is perceived intuitively. It can also mean that even as actual cognition the abstractive depends on the intuitive, at least in so far as the initial abstractive acts are concerned, from which possibly the habitual can stem.

If the first view is accepted, namely, that only as habitual knowledge does the abstractive depend on the intuitive, then the question arises whether intuitive acts can produce abstractive habits. The positive answer to this question had its appealing aspects for Ockham, as was noted above.[19] First, it represented a simple solution to the problem, since it required no intermediary factor, and this to his mind was no small advantage. Secondly, it seemed in accord with certain facts of observation which did not indicate the presence of an initial abstractive act accompanying the intuitive acts. As a matter of fact this fictitious initial abstractive act seemed to be

---

[17] Potest tamen intellectus postea abstrahere multa et conceptus communes formare, intelligendo unum conceptorum in re, non intelligendo reliquum; et hoc non potest competere sensui.

Si autem ista abstractio intelligitur universaliter, intelligenda est ex parte intellectionis, quia illa est simpliciter immaterialis; non sic autem de cognitione sensitiva.—Ord. Prol. I, TT.

[18] Secundo dico quod cognitio simplex propria singularis et prima tali primitate (*generationis*) est cognitio intuitiva. Quod autem illa sit prima patet quia cognitio singularis abstractiva praesupponit intuitivam respectu eiusdem objecti, et non econtra.—Quodl. I, 13.—Cf. Ord. Prol. I, Z.

[19] Page 21.

opposed to the facts of experience, for whereas all abstractive acts can persist after the object has been removed, this one does not seem to be able to do this.[20]

That this explanation had its advantages in the eyes of Ockham can also be seen by the fact that he tried to answer certain objections against it. The most serious one arose out of Aristotelian principles governing habit-formation.[21] According to this, habits always reproduce acts similar to those which produced them. And thus, intuitive cognition could not produce habits which would cause abstractive acts.

In answering this objection, Ockham tried an evasion by offering a convenient interpretation of Aristotle's principle. He suggested that its application be limited to cases where the acts are the total causes of the habit, and not extended to those where they are only the partial causes. Intuitive acts with regard to abstractive habits was a case in point, he thought. And indeed intuitive acts would not be more than partial causes. But what acts are more than partial causes of any habit?[22] Was it not explained above that the concurrence of the potency is always required?[23]

Whatever the value of this theory in itself or in the eyes of Ockham when it was elaborated, it does not seem to have left any

---

[20] Aliter potest dici quod habitus generatur ex cognitione intuitiva sicut ex causa partiali et negari cognitio abstractiva quae simul ponitur cum intuitiva; tum quia nullus experitur quod simul et semel cognoscat eandem rem intuitive et abstractive, et hoc loquendo de cognitione abstractiva rei in se. Immo potius experitur homo oppositum, maxime cum illae cognitiones habeant aliquas conditiones oppositas; tum quia omnis cognitio abstractiva potest manere, destructa intuitiva, ista autem quae ponitur non potest manere. —Rep. II, 14-15, K.

[21] Nic. Eth. II, 1103a, 34.

[22] Cf. ante p. 8.

[23] Si dicis quod habitus secundum Philosophum, secundo Ethicorum, inclinat ad actus consimiles ex quibus generatur et non ad actus alterius rationis, sicut est in proposito de cognitione intuitiva et abstractiva, respondeo: verum est generaliter quando habitus non generatur ex cognitione intuitiva tamquam ex causa partiali. Sed quando cognitio intuitiva est causa partialis, sicut est in proposito tunc non est verum. Minus enim inconveniens apparet quod habitus inclinans ad cognitionem abstractivam generatur ex cognitione intuitiva tamquam ex causa partiali, quam quod cum intuitiva maneat semper cognitio abstractiva generativa habitum, cum tamen experientia non sit ad hoc sed potius ad oppositum.—Rep. II, 14-15, L.

trace in his subsequent thinking, as was said above.[24] On the other hand, the opposite view, namely that intuitive cognition produces no habit, at least directly,[25] is held consistenly and formed the basis of subsequent theorization.[26]

If, therefore, intuitive cognition cannot cause habitual abstractive knowledge directly, an intermediary factor must be posited in order to maintain the causal link between the two. In other words, the dependence of abstractive cognition on intuitive perception is such that initial abstractive acts, capable of producing the abstractive habits, must be posited and linked causally with the intuitive acts, notwithstanding the fact that their presence is not directly observable nor warranted by certain data of experience, as Ockham remarked. They are posited here as theoretical, necessary factors to explain habits, if the general theory of habit is to be maintained. The intuitive acts are therefore said to cause the initial abstractive acts. Since the former are fleeting and transitory, it follows that the latter must occur practically simultaneously with them. Hence Ockham's expression "simul et semel."[27]

The causal connection between this *prima abstractiva*, as the initial theoretical abstractive act is called, and the intuitive acts is carefully described by Ockham. All the contributing factors are mentioned. Besides the intuitive act itself, he indicates as causes of the *prima abstractiva* the intellect and the body (corpore). Obviously, by saying that the body is partial cause he is referring to his tenet that sense intuitive acts are partial causes of the intellective intuitive.[28]

---

[24] Cf. ante p. 22.

[25] Reference was made above to Hochstetter's contention that Ockham continued to maintain that habits are produced by intuitive acts directly and to Boehner's opposite stand. Cf. p. 22, n. 12.

[26] . . . ex nulla cognitione intuitiva sensitiva vel intellectiva potest generari habitus; quia si sic, aut ille habitus inclinat ad cognitionem abstractivam aut intuitivam. Non abstractivam, propter causam iam dictam, quia sunt alterius speciei; nec intuitivam, quia nullus experitur quod magis inclinatur ad cognitionem intuitivam post talem cognitionem frequenter habitam quam ante.— Rep. II, 14-15, H.

[27] Et hic est notandum quod, stante cognitione intuitiva alicuius rei, habeo simul et semel cognitionem abstractivam eiusdem rei.—Rep. II, 14-15, G. (For causal link see note 30).

[28] Quodl. I, 15.

Indirectly therefore at least, the senses, or the body, would be causes of the abstractive. But the causal effect of the object on the abstractive act is still more remote. In fact, Ockham corrects an earlier view[29] on this point and denies any causal link between the object and the abstractive: "licet contrarium prius dicatur." The reason is that the abstractive can be produced as long as the intuitive exists, irrespective of the presence or absence of the object. However by comparison with the earlier text, it can be seen that only the direct causal link is here objected to, since that seemed to be implied in the earlier view, and since the indirect link through the intuitive act is obviously not denied. The object is, naturally speaking, necessary for all intuitive acts, and intuitive acts are necessary for the *prima abstractiva*.[30]

Once the *prima abstractiva* is established, abstractive habits, or habitual abstractive knowledge becomes possible. The subsequent acts are replicas of the *prima*. The original experiences are recalled through the dynamic power of habit in collaboration with the intellect. Neither intuitive acts nor the presence of the object are required for these revived experiences. These are also *incomplex* acts and can serve as bases of judgments in a manner similar to the *prima*.[31]

Though habit is possible after the first abstractive act, Ockham does not hold that one act is always sufficient for the establishment of a habit. It can happen, he explains, that the trace left by the first act be entirely effaced by forgetting. The same can happen to that of the second and third, and so forth. There is nothing in his theory opposed to this. But in that case it is always the precise act which

---

[29] Probably a reference to Ord. I, d.27, q.3, where it is said: "Ita nihil est medium inter objectum et notitiam abstractivam."

[30] Circa notitiam primam abstractivam, quae simul stat cum intuitive, est advertendum quod illa notitia causetur ab intuitiva notitia et intellectu et corpore, quodcumque sit illud, tamquam a causis partialibus, et non ab objecto, licet contrarium prius dicatur. Cuius ratio est quia stante cognitione intuitiva et objecto toto corrupto adhuc stat illa abstractiva. Ergo non requiritur objectum necessario ad eius causationem.—Rep. II, 16, GG.

[31] Loquendo vero de notitia abstractiva tunc aut loquimur de illa quae semper consequitur intuitivam aut de illa quae habetur post corruptionem intuitivae . . . Si secundo modo loquimur, sic ad illam requiritur intellectus et habitus generatus ex cognitione abstractiva elicita simul cum intuitiva, et non requiritur objectum in ista secunda cognitione abstractiva tamquam causa partialis (*mediata*), quia illa potest haberi etiam si objectum annihiletur. Et est utraque istarum notitiarum abstractivarum incomplexa.—Rep. II, 14-15, U.

originates the habit, or originates it anew, that is considered the *prima abstractiva*, speaking technically. That act, whether in reality it be the fifth or hundredth, requires the presence of the intuitive act as the cause, that is, partial cause, of its existence. After the habit is formed and as long as it remains operative, the intuitive act is no longer necessary.[32]

Reviewing the facts about the cognitive processes, so far discussed, we recall that Ockham's great preoccupation was to assure an objective basis for all our knowledge. As far as actual knowledge was concerned, no great difficulty presented itself. He posited the perception of the singular object by intuitive cognition as the source of .this type of knowledge. Regarding habitual knowledge, however, greater difficulties were experienced. We began by distinguishing two main species of this kind of knowledge. Besides that representing existential or contingent facts, there is that viewing reality as divested of contingent conditions such as the *hic et nunc* existence or non-existence or any other accidental determination. From there we proceeded to explain how the latter, both as habitual and actual knowledge, could satisfactorily be linked with the former, namely, intuitive perception. In describing this link for the habitual form, habits were postulated, and to justify these the notion of the *prima abstractiva* had to be introduced. In laying the foundations of habitual abstractive knowledge, Ockham prepared the ground for a discussion of memory, for habitual knowledge is knowledge that can be recalled. But the first type of cognition described, namely, knowledge of contingent circumstances, can also become habitual in the sense of being subject to later recall by memory. How this can be explained will be made clear in the section on memory.

---

[32] Nam si habitus derelicti a prima abstractiva, secunda, tertia, quarta, corrumpuntur per oblivionem, sicut est possibile, tamen ad hoc quinta abstractiva eliciatur naturaliter necessario praesupponit intuitivam tamquam causam eius partialem, quia omne derelictum ab abstractivis prioribus per positum est corruptum. Et sic non necessario requirant causas alterius rationis prima abstractiva et secunda, quia ambae possunt fieri a causa eiusdem rationis. Tamen prima abstractiva necessario requirit aliam causam alterius rationis quod, si naturaliter causatur, non requirit secunda, quia prima requirit intuitivam, naturaliter loquendo, secunda non necessario quia licet in priori casu requirat necessario intuitivam, non tamen abstractiva secunda quia potest fieri mediante habitu derelicto a prima abstractiva, posito quod maneat.—Rep. II, 16, Z.

3. IN MEMORY

Memory is a complex process and does not easily lend itself to analytic description. However, Ockham's views on this point can best be understood, it seems, by distinguishing in memory three steps or moments. There is first the basic factor of retention, for we must assume our experiences leave behind them certain psychological marks or traces if we are to explain the possibility of recall. Secondly, there is the ability to remember the individual features of the objects or persons we knew and thus recognize them later. This we shall term recognition. Thirdly there is the ability to remember the fact itself of having had such and such an experience in the past. This shall be termed recall.

Retention

At the basis of retention, according to Ockham, is habit-formation. Habit is that trace left by experiences of the past by which they may be recalled. But habit is more than an inert mark or trace. It is a dynamic factor which contributes actively to make recall possible. Ockham explains this by saying that, whereas in the initial act the active concurrence of the object known was necessary to produce the knowledge act, in the revived experience the object is not required, and its influence is replaced by a new factor, namely, habit.[33]

Equally basic to the notion of retention is the element of intentionality. A trace must be a trace of something; it must have meaning, that is, it must direct the mind away from itself to something it stands for and signifies. So also the acts revived by habit must represent something, apart from being revived psychological experiences.

Ockham had this problem clearly in mind when he elaborated

---

[33] Quantum ad tertiam difficultatem dico quod memoria dupliciter accipitur: uno modo pro potentia habente aliquem habitum vel qualitatem derelictum ex actu praeterito, virtute cuius potest talis potentia in aliquem actum consimilem et eiusdem rationis cum actu praeterito, qui quidem actus praeteritus aliquod requirit ad suum esse quod non exigitur ad esse secundi actus, puta objectum extra.—Rep. IV, 12, J.

his habit-theory. His definitive solution[34] was to identify the intentionality or meaningfulness of the intellection with the psychological act itself. Thus by its very nature the initial act signified the object known, and thus the revived act could inherit, so to speak, this same prerogative. It lost none of its intentionality by being removed from actual consciousness in point of time or by being consigned to memory and later reproduced by habit. It could not only signify the object, but could serve as the basis of *complex* acts, or judgments. Furthermore it could signify other psychological acts and play the part of a genus or species with regard to first intention notions. In a word, concludes Ockham, it is capable of every function that can be performed by the *fictum*,[35] which is postulated by some as a product of the psychological act and to which is assigned the task of signifying the object known.[36]

Retention is explained, therefore, on the basis of habit-formation. But as was seen in the first two sections of this chapter, the only possible cognitive habits are abstractive. Now abstractive cognition is characterized by its ability to abstract from the contingent circumstances of existence or non-existence, and so forth. How then can it serve as a medium of recall of individual experiences? How can it call to mind the knowledge of a singular object or person?

Recognition

The truth is, Ockham admits, that no simple, elemental abstractive act, or concept (and these two are synonymous), can signify or represent an individual, singular object. The concepts of abstractive cognition which first come to mind in connection with a specific object are simple but not proper to this object alone. The Venerabilis

---

[34] There seems to be strong evidence, according to Philotheus Boehner, that at one time Ockham favoured another theory, namely the fictum theory. See: Philotheus Boehner, *The Realistic Conceptualism of William Ockham* (Traditio, New York, IV, 1946) pp. 307-319.

[35] For Ockham's own description of the *fictum* and other theories see Ord. I, d. 2. q. 8, E. This *fictum* is very much like the *species* with which the reader is more familiar. More than that need not be said here.

[36] Ideo dico quod tam intentio prima quam secunda sunt vere actus intelligendi. Potest salvari quidquid salvatur per fictum eo quod actus est similitudo objecti et potest significare et supponere pro rebus extra. Potest esse subjectum et praedicatum in propositione; potest esse genus et species, etc. sicut fictum.—Quodl. IV, 35.

Inceptor refers to the testimony of experience for confirmation of this point. On seeing a strange object from a distance, a person would normally first qualify the object as a *thing*. Thereby he records his perception of that object in the most general concept possible. Only when this is done, can the observer give it a more definite classification, and call it a house or an animal for instance. In any case the first concepts, in the order of generation, are the most general and are not proper to the individual object.[37]

Nay more, it is against the very nature of elemental abstractive acts or concepts to signify or represent individual things or persons. Hence they cannot represent one individual more than another which is like it. But they do represent them all equally, and thus the factor of intentionality is still maintained. However no elemental or simple concept is proper to an individual object but is universal by its very nature.[38]

How the mind proceeds from these universal ideas to others which are increasingly more particular is explained by Ockham as the result of a natural process of the mind. For him there is nothing *a priori* about the classification of beings into genera and species. It is not deducible from any established order in the world; nor can it be proven as necessary *a posteriori*. It is simply a matter of observation, dependent on intuitive cognition of things as they are.[39]

No *a priori* character can be attributed to them because of the

---

[37] Dico tertio quod cognitio prima abstractiva, primitate generationis, et simplex non est cognitio propria singulari, sed est communis.

Prima pars patet quia non habetur cognitio propria simplex de aliquo singulari pro tempore pro quo non potest haberi cognitio eius specifica sive generalis. Quod autem sit ita patet de veniente a remotis quod causat talem sensationem virtute cuius tantum possum iudicare quod illud visum est ens. Notum est quod in illo casu cognitio abstractiva quam habeo primo, primitate generationis, est cognitio entis et nullius inferioris, et per consequens non est conceptus specificus nec est conceptus proprius singulari.—Quodl, I, 13.

[38] Secunda pars patet quia nulla cognitio abstractiva simplex est plus similitudo unius rei singularis quam alterius sibi simillimae, nec causatur a re nec nata est causari. Ergo nulla talis est propria singularis, sed quaelibet est universalis.—*Ibid.*—Cf. Quodl. V, 7.

[39] Prima pars definitionis, puta genus nec a priori nec a posteriori potest demonstrari a definito; sicut quod homo sit animal demonstrari non potest, sed propositio talis sine sillogismo acquiritur, mediante notitia intuitiva.—Sum. Log. III, 2, c. 29, p. 71.

admitted fact that generic ideas are in the developed mind available for the description of hitherto unclassified objects. That they remain unchanged in the mind does not mean that they precede all intuitive contact with the world, nor that they were not the fruit of a developing mind. It would seem that Ockham considered the formation of these general concepts a part of man's early training, since he intimates that the memory of their acquisition is not always so vivid that no doubt can be had about their origin.[40]

He reconstitutes the development of the general notions that go to make up our definition of man. At the origin he places an intuitive act of sense cognition, followed by an intuitive act of intellective cognition. From this perception of a human being results a general concept, common to all men. The more general notion that he is *something, a being* (*ens*), is also conceived by the observer and at the same time. Next we suppose the observer perceives one or more animals, other than the rational *animal*. Immediately in his mind there is formed a concept common to all animals, including the rational. When this is done, the intellect can compare the two notions in their application to man. The proposition that man is both an animal and a rational being is formed spontaneously in the mind. Assent can be given to it as to any other proposition without the need of discourse. Therefore, common concepts like genus, species, etc. are the result of observation and the natural process which we have termed integration[41] in our discussion of the general characteristics of habit.[42]

The process of integration goes on far beyond the definition stage. More and more simple concepts are gathered together in the

---

[40] Unde istis conceptibus existentibus in intellectu et aliquo homine viso, statim scitur quod homo est animal, non quod isti conceptus praecedant notitiam intuitivam hominis.—*Ibid.*

[41] Chap. I, p. 13.

[42] Sed iste est processus: quod primo homo cognoscitur aliquo sensu particulari, deinde idem homo cognoscitur ab intellectu. Quo cognito, habetur notitia generalis et communis omni homini . . . Quo (*conceptu*) existente in intellectu, statim intellectus scit quod homo est aliquo sine discursu. Deinde apprehenso aliquo animali, alio ab homine, vel aliis animalibus elicitur una notitia generais, et ista notitia generalis est communis omni animali . . . Quo existente in anima potest intellectus componere istum conceptum cum conceptu priori. Quibus compositis ad invicem, mediante hoc verbo *est*, statim intellectus assentit illi complexo sine omni sillogismo.— Sum. Log. *1b.*

mind until the agglomeration formed is a representation of an individual, singular object or person. This unified concept is called a proper concept and is the basis of recognition of things or persons known previously. Besides the basic intentionality of each simple, elemental concept which it contains, it possesses a sort of collective intentionality relating it to one object and one object or person alone. The latter it derives from its distinctive nature, that is, a configuration of elements such that it cannot be duplicated, no more than one being in objective reality is a duplication of another. Thus, to use Ockham's illustration, I can remember having known Socrates because my remembrance of him brings with it the memory of his size, colour, shape and the environment in which I met him. The Venerabilis Inceptor suggests that if all but one of the elemental notions be abstracted from this composite mental picture of Socrates, I would no longer be able to say if it was really Socrates I saw or someone else, say Plato. Thus, he concludes that abstractive concepts can serve as a medium of recall and recognition of past experiences. Composite concepts can recall singular experiences but elemental concepts can recall only common data. The number and the kind of elemental notions assembled in one composite notion are such that they are applicable to only one objective being.[43]

This composite act, it goes without saying, can produce a habit which assures it retention and reproduction. This is in accord with Ockham's general principle which states that when elemental acts can cause habits then the composite acts of the same nature can do so likewise.[44] In this case both are abstractive acts.

Thus far, concerning the process of memory, we have described the factor of retention and recognition. We have explained that

---

[43] Ad tertium dico quod, videndo aliquid, habeo aliquam cognitionem abstractivam propriam; sed illa non est simplex, sed composita ex simplicibus. Et illa notitia composita est principium recordationis. Et per hoc recordor de Sorte quia vidi eum sic, vel figuratum, coloratum, talis longitudinis, latitudinis, et in tali loco; et per illum conceptum recordor me vidisse Sortem. Patet quia si circumscribas omnes conceptus simplices praeter unum, non plus recordareris de Sorte per illum quam de alio homine sibi simillimo. Bene possum recordari me vidisse, sed utrum sit Sortes vel Plato nescio. Et ideo cognitio abstractiva simplex non est propria singulari, sed composita bene potest esse propria.—Quodl. I, 13.

[44] Chap. 1, p. 14.

the traces left by past experiences are really habits, and how such habits can retain and reproduce complete mental pictures of individual objects or persons. But the question may be asked, how do we know that the mental picture we have of a thing at present was really formed at the time of the perception of the thing. In other words, is there a way of recognizing a past experience as such independently of mental picture-content? Ockham contends that there is and sets about describing it.

Recall

The word *recall* is used here to signify that factor of the process of memory whereby we are able to recognize experiences of the past as such, irrespective of the ability or inability to describe them or to describe the objects connected with them. Ockham considers this factor an integral part of the process of remembering.[45]

In describing this function of memory, Ockham begins by what he considers its fundamental elements. At the root of recall, according to him, there is perception which provides evidence concerning existence or non-existence or other contingent elements. Would this be intuitive cognition? Yes, except for the fact that the existence or non-existence, etc., in this case refer to past time. The similarity, however, impresses Ockham; so he calls it with Scotus imperfect intuitive cognition, reserving the term *perfect* for that relating to present events, as described in section one of this chapter. Both provide evidence for existential judgments or propositions: the perfect for *hic et nunc* facts or events, the imperfect for facts known now to have existed in the past.[46]

The difference between the imperfect and the perfect intuitive cognitions is reflected in Ockham's account of their etiology or genesis. Whereas according to him the latter cannot be effected,

---

[45] . . . illa potentia quae potest cognoscere actum suum esse praeteritum vel praecessisse habet memoriam propriam dictam. Sed intellectus est huiusmodi. —Rep. IV, 12, J.

[46] Sed intuitiva subdividitur quia quaedam est perfecta, quaedam imperfecta. Perfecta cognitio intuitiva est illa de qua dictum est quod est cognitio experimentalis, qua cognosco rem esse, etc . . . Cognitio autem intuitiva imperfecta est illa per quam iudicamus rem aliquando fuisse vel non fuisse, et haec dicitur cognitio recordativa.—Rep. II, 14-15, G.

normally speaking, except in the presence of the object, the former does not require the presence of the object.[47]

This feature of imperfect intuitive cognition of being producible without the concurrence of any object shows that it is similar to the abstractive form of cognition. Ockham notes this similarity and observes that, because of this, the imperfect intuitive can be called abstractive cognition. However, he adds, since the knowledge it furnishes contains a reference to time and existence, it can be termed intuitive, that is, imperfect intuitive, because the reference is to past existence.[48]

Retention of a past experience even when it contains a time-reference is explained on the basis of habit-formation. The problem presenting itself is that of integrating this new factor, imperfect intuitive cognition, into the closely knit structure of cognitive habits. At the basis of these habits, it will be recalled, Ockham had postulated a *prima abstractiva* produced by, and existing concomitantly with initial intuitive acts. If the imperfect intuitive is to be considered a product of habit, then it must be linked with habits caused by the *prima abstractiva*. To bolster this view, Ockham refers to empirical evidence. Observation reveals that immediately after the intuitive perceptive act we are able to refer to this cognitive experience as a thing of the past. It must be assumed, therefore, that habit-formation began at the time of the intuitive act. But since, as we know, the intuitive act itself cannot cause any habit, the causality must stem directly from the *prima abstractiva*, which for that reason must be contemporaneous with the intuitive act. Retention of experiences

---

[47] Ex dictis apparet differentia inter cognitionem intuitivam perfectam et imperfectam, quia prima non est nec potest esse naturaliter, nisi objectum existat; secunda potest esse, etsi objectum destruatur.—*Ib.* M.

[48] Si dicas quod cognitio intuitiva imperfecta est simpliciter abstractiva quia abstrahit ab existentia rei, ergo non est intuitiva, respondeo: pro tanto dicitur intuitiva quia mediante ea potest intellectus assentire alicui complexo quod concernit differentiam temporis, puta quod hoc fuit, sicut per intuitivam perfectam potest iudicare quod hoc est . . .

Ideo licet illa cognitio, per quam iudico rem aliquando fuisse sit simpliciter abstractiva, quia tamen mediante ea assentio et iudico rem aliquando fuisse et non mediantibus aliis cognitionibus, ideo respectu earum potest dici cognitio intuitiva, imperfecta tamen.—*Ibid.*

with definite time-reference has a common origin with those having no time-reference.[49]

Though stemming from a common origin, the retained and recalled imperfect intuitive act and the ordinary abstractive act have not the same content or object. That of the former may be said to be more extensive and to include that of the latter; or it may be said to have a double object, one of which may be identical with that of the former and the other containing the reported time-element.[50]

In fact however, the individual *prima abstractiva* which renders possible the retention of knowledge without time-reference is not the same as that which renders possible knowledge with time-reference. In the latter case Ockham postulates a reflexive act of the intellect upon the original act, which therefore forms the direct object of the cognition involving time-reference. No external or objective thing or event is the immediate object of recall in this strict sense of the word. Thus what one remembers, strictly speaking, is not the action of some other person whom one may have heard speaking or seen writing, etc. It is rather one's own subjective experiences caused by these objective phenomena. In view of this, Ockham distinguishes between the act which is remembered (actus recordantis) and the act which remembers (actus recordandi). The acts remembered can be any cognitive act, intuitive and abstractive, as well as any act of the will and the sensitive powers.[51]

---

[49] Et est hic notandum quod, stante cognitione intuitiva alicuius rei, habeo simul et semel cognitionem eiusdem rei. Et illa cognitio abstractiva est causa partialis concurrens cum intellectu ad generandum habitum inclinantem ad cognitionem intuitivam imperfectam, per quam iudico rem aliquando fuisse . . .

Ergo si habitus inclinans ad cognitionem intuitivam imperfectam generetur ex aliquo actu cognitivo, illa cognitio erit abstractiva, et illa erit simul cum cognitione intuitiva perfecta, quia statim post cognitionem intuitivam perfectam, sive objectum destruatur, sive sit absens, potest intellectus eandem rem, quam prius vidit intuitive, considerare et formare hoc complexum: haec res aliquando fuit; et assentire evidenter, sicut quilibet experitur in seipso.—Rep. II, 14-15, G.

[50] Unde dico quod actus recordandi habet duplex objectum, scil. partiale et totale. Partiale est actus recordantis praeteritus . . . totale, complexum puta propositio composita ex actu recordantis et termino significante tempus praeteritum.—Rep. IV, 12, H.

[51] . . . partiale (objectum) est actus recordantis praeteritus, et potest esse

But these subjective acts are only the partial objects of real acts of recall. The total object includes a psychological element, which serves as the other term of the judgment of recall. Its function is to refer to past time and it identifies these acts as having occurred before. Therefore, the act of remembering in its complete reality is a complex act or judgment, which is usually expressed in such formulas as: I saw this; I heard that; or I heard John read on such and such a day. Thus, the object of remembering, as viewed here, is a composite object and the act itself is a judgment.[52]

In the act of remembering the composite object is viewed by Ockham as being present to the intellect. The judgment ensuing is based on evidence concerning this object, which is no more, of course, than a recalled act plus its time-reference. The act furnishing the evidence is an act of imperfect intuitive cognition. This presupposes a perfect intuitive act at some time in the past, because Ockham links the possibility of recalling an act with a time-reference to a reflexive awareness of this same act when it occurred originally under the influence of the objective reality.[53]

To the reflexive awareness of an act at the time when it occurs originally Ockham links a special habit. This is a composite habit because the object it retains is the direct act plus the time-reference. This habit, born of a *complex* act which asserts that such an act now exists for the first time, will later be instrumental in producing judgments to the effect that this act, now recalled, existed in the past.

---

intuitivus vel abstractivus, in intellectu vel in potentia sensitiva, vel in voluntate vel in appetitu sensitivo. Non enim objectum partiale immediatum est actus alterius a recordante, puta actus loquendi, vel disputandi, vel scribendi alterius hominis; quia de talibus non recordor nisi quatenus me recordor audivisse vel vidisse eum talia facere, ita quod actus meus quem sum recordans aliquando terminabatur ad illos actus disputandi, legendi, etc.—*Ibid.*

[52] Objectum primum totale respectu actus recordandi est quidam complexum, puta propositio quaedam composita ex actu recordantis tamquam ex objecto partiali et ex alio termino significante vel consignificante tempus praeteritum, puta ista: hoc vidi, hoc audivi; audivi Johannem tali die legere; et actus terminatus ad istud complexum est actus recordandi.—*Ibid.*

[53] Ad aliud dico quod illud complexum est evidenter notum; et dico quod illa notitia est evidens notitia qua intellectus evidenter ·assentit huic complexo: hoc vidi, hoc audivi, hoc intellexi. (*Illa notitia*) causatur ex notitia intuitiva terminorum, (*i.e.*) intuitiva imperfecta terminorum. Et haec praesupponit, naturaliter loquendo, intuitivam perfectam.—Rep. IV, 12, Q.

Hence an additional habit, which is a *complex* habit, is postulated by Ockham to explain the complete process of memory.[54]

That this habit should be caused by a judgment asserting some-thing is, and then produce judgments asserting something *was*, is not considered a violation of the theory of habit-formation. The change in the time-reference does not, according to Ockham, affect the nature of the habit involved.[55]

The *complex* habit, though more immediately. responsible for the act of recall, as described here, does not function in complete independence from *incomplex* or elemental habits. Indeed, acts retained by these simpler habits can become embodied in the broader ones at any time, on condition that notice of their existence is taken by a reflexive intuitive cognition, from which the *complex* habits spring.[56]

However, remembering properly so called, according to Ock-ham, refers to the *complex* acts and the *complex* habits, whereby awareness of a subjective experience is first expressed and then retained for later recall.[57]

Reviewing these paragraphs on recall, it will be remembered that its point of departure is the reflexive act whereby cognizance is taken by perfect intuitive cognition of an original experience. Habit is then postulated to retain this first judgment of awareness. When

---

[54] . . . .(*intellectus*) intuitive videt actum suum, et potest tunc cognoscere evidenter quod actus suus est, et ex illo actu complexo evidenti generatur habitus inclinans ad cognoscendum evidenter quod iste actus fuit . . . *Ib.* J.

[55] Sic non solum habuit recordans illum actum incomplexúm generativum habitus incomplexi, sed etiam actum complexum duplicem: unum quo apprehendit illum actum esse et alium quo evidenter assentit huic complexo, iste actus est. Et ex isto actu generatur habitus complexus inclinans immediate ad actum recordandi, similem sibi in specie, saltem quantum ad principale objectum qui est actus recordantis, licet mutetur differentia temporis quae non mutat speciem habitus.—*Ib.* P.

[56] Ad aliam rationem pro dubio dico quod primus actus recordandi causatur ab habitu complexo immediate et ab habitu vel habitibus incomplexis mediate tamen, quia quando actus recordantis fuit est objectum partiale actus recordandi.—*Ibid.*

[57] Alio modo (*memoria*) accipitur pro potentia quae potest in actum recordandi proprie dictum mediante habitu genito ex actibus praeteritis, non quidem incomplexis sed complexis.—Rep. IV, 12, J.

the retained act is reproduced, it is cognized by imperfect intuitive cognition. This affords evidence not only about the content of the act but about its temporal characteristic. On the basis of this evidence a judgment is formed to express awareness that the revived experience is remembered as such. This is in addition to the content of the experience which is the same as that of the original. For greater clarity an attempt shall be made to represent the successive stages of this process in schematic form on a separate page.

4. IN FORGETTING

Forgetting is viewed by Ockham as the destruction of acquired habits as a result of long disuse. To quote an example he gives, one can forget how a certain proposition is demonstrated if one does not review the proof from time to time.

Seeking the cause of this destruction, the Venerabilis Inceptor first gives a very broad and general explanation, which is however quite characteristic of his thinking. According to it, habit is destroyed because God, the first cause, ceases to conserve it when there is no continued use made of it by repeated actions on the part of the subject.[58]

---

[58] Primum (*dubium*) est de corruptibilitate habitus . . . quia potest corrumpi per cessationem actuum longo tempore, sicut aliquis obliviscit demonstrationem alicuius conclusionis quam iam prius scivit propter defectum exercitii.

Ad primum istorum potest dici quod Deus non conservat quando deficit exercitium actus diu, et tunc corrumpuntur.—*Ib.* L.

PROCESS OF RECALL

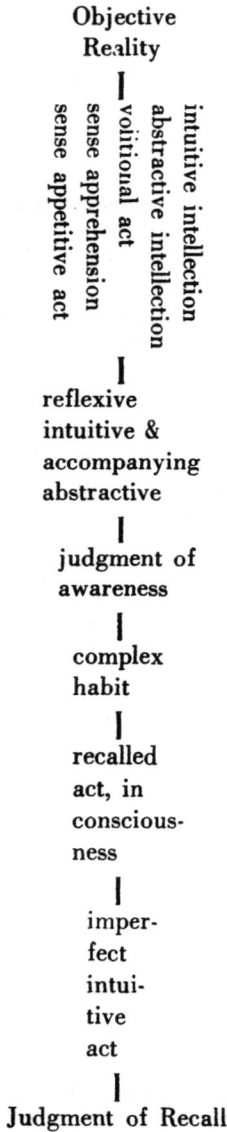

Objective
Reality

|

intuitive intellection
abstractive intellection
volitional act
sense apprehension
sense appetitive act

|

reflexive
intuitive &
accompanying
abstractive

|

judgment of
awareness

|

complex
habit

|

recalled
act, in
conscious-
ness

|

imper-
fect
intui-
tive
act

|

Judgment of Recall

This explanation of forgetting is based on the principle that habits are produced and conserved by the same cause or causes, namely human acts and God. And indeed, no other cause is required, strictly speaking. In theory therefore bodily dispositions should have no influence on memory.[59]

In fact however, the effect of physiological conditions on memory in undeniable. Ockham accepted this fact and quoted Aristotle's Categories as proof that the Greek Philosopher held a similar view.[60] From this the Venerabilis Inceptor concludes that there is some link between bodily dispositions and the conservation of intellectual habits.[61]

Not only dispositions brought about by illness, according to Ockham, can have an effect on memory. There are also those which seemed to be produced in the body as a result of repeated acts of intellection and volition in the soul. Thus if the intellect under the influence of the will continuously restrains the passions and the urges of the sensitive powers, a permanent or quasi-permanent character seems to be impressed in the dispositions of the body which is favourable to the conservation of habits in the intellect and will. The destruction of these dispositions results in the deterioration of these mental habits.[62]

---

[59] . . . ex eisdem causis generantur actus et habitus, et conservantur, quia posita causa sufficienti generativa et conservativa habitus potest poni habitus, circumscripto quocumque alio. Sed circumscripta omni dispositione corporali, posito solo intellectu cum objecto, ponitur causa generativa sufficiens tam actus quam habitus. Igitur circumscripta tali dispositione, potest habitus prius acquisitus conservari.—Rep. IV, 12, C.

[60] Cat. 8, 8b, 30.

[61] Eodem modo tam habitus illi quam actus mediante tali dispositione conservantur; et propter eius defectum corrumpuntur, sicut patet per Philosophum in Praedicamentis quo dicit quod per longam infirmitatem potest scientia prius acquisita diminui vel totaliter corrumpi. Hoc docet experientia manifeste.—Rep. *Ib.*

[62] Aliter potest dici quod ex actibus intellectus frequenter elicitis causatur aliqua qualitas in corpore, et voluntate similiter, sicut videmus quod actus concupiscentiae, sive passiones appetitus sensitivi moderantur per actus intelligendi et volendi per hoc quod voluntas suspendit actum intellectus respectu talium, et convertit se ad alia, et voluntas vult Deum vel aliquid tale; ita quod ex frequenti intellectione et volitione potest generari et augeri aliqua qualitas corporalis quae est conservans habitum in intellectu et voluntate, sive quia frequenter secundum alterationem animae sequitur alteratio corporis. Et

There are also positive factors having a destructive influence on these bodily dispositions, such as the elements and other external forces. Unless their influence is continuously counteracted by the repetition of acts on the part of the intellectual powers, these external forces can bring about the complete destruction of the knowledge habits. Thus, says Ockham, it can be explained how through the cessation of mental activity, habits in the intellect and will can be destroyed.[63]

II. On The Sense Level

Cognition on the sense level does not only refer to knowledge registered by the five senses, as sight, hearing, etc., but includes knowledge by the faculty known as the imagination (phantasia). In Ockham's system there is an organic unity between the two cognitive powers or groups of powers. The former are called the external and the latter the internal senses. Both are dependent on one single form, the sensitive form, which is really distinct from the intellective form.[64]

To grasp the role assigned by Ockham to habit in this intricate cognitive structure, it is necessary to consider, at least briefly, his description of the two distinct processes involved. Beginning with the external senses: sight, hearing, etc., he gives a precise description of the actual sensation by differentiating it from the accompanying physiological phenomena. Of these he distinguishes two.

---

ideo ad corruptionem illius qualitatis corporalis conservantis sequitur corruptio habitus in anima.—Rep. IV, 12, L.

[63] Illa autem qualitas corporalis corrumpitur per actionem extrinsecorum agentium, qui continue agunt in corpus, alterando diversimodo. Cuiusmodi sunt elementa et alia corpora multa propter quorum actionem corrumpitur qualitas illa corporalis quando non augetur per frequentationem actuum intellectus et voluntatis. Et haec videtur esse ratio quare corrumpitur habitus in intellectu et voluntate per cessationem actuum; et dicitur esse corruptio per oblivionem.—*Ibid.*

[64] . . . sed tota forma sensitiva in homine est una forma, licet habeat partes diversas extensas sub diversis partibus quantitatis; ideo respectu unius objecti sufficit cognitio intuitiva unius potentiae illius formae, et respectu alterius sufficit cognitio intuitiva alterius potentiae eiusdem formae, sicut patet de sensibilibus quinque sensuum exteriorum; et ideo omnes cognitiones potentiarum interiorum eiusdem formae sunt abstractivae, et propter rationem eandem quia anima intellectiva distinguitur in homine realiter a sensitiva.—Rep. II, 17, Q.

The first is a certain stimulating or irritating effect on the sense organs by the object. In Aristotle,[65] to whom Ockham refers, we find the following description of this phenomenon. ". . . after strong stimulation of a sense we are less able to exercise it than before, as for instance in the case of a bright colour or a powerful odour we cannot see or smell . . . The reason is that while the faculty of sensation is dependent upon the body, mind is separable from it."

The second physical effect of the object on the senses is a certain likeness of itself produced in them. In the case of sight, for instance, it is an image of the object which is imprinted in the eyes and remains there for some time. It is perceptible even after the object has been removed, as for instance when one closes one's eyes after having viewed a bright object. This impression, says Ockham, is a positive quality produced by the object at the same time as the actual sensation is caused, but is neither the cause nor the effect of the sensation or act by which the object is actually known. The reason given is that this effect of the object, like the one described in the preceding paragraph resides in the sense organ and not in the sensitive potency which is the centre of all sense-cognition.[66]

The third and last effect of the object, at least as a partial cause, is the act of seeing or hearing itself. This resides in the potency itself and not in the sense organs; though their instrumentality is essential to the acquisition of the awareness.[67]

---

[65] On The Soul, III, 4, 429b, 1.

[66] Quantum ergo ad potentias exteriores recapitulando dico quod in visu imprimitur quaedam qualitas confortans vel debilitans organum, et illa est subjective in organo quia organum debilitatur et non potentia, sicut patet per Philosophum, primo Animae . . .

Praeter istam qualitatem est ponere unam aliam quae est passio vel passibilis qualitas quae potest sentiri a sensu, et ista est eiusdem rationis cum objecto extra, et imprimitur simul cum primo actu videndi aliquod sensibile excellens et non generatur ex illo actu nec est principium illius actus, sicut nec alia qualitas debilitans. Sed utraque istarum simul imprimitur in organo visus distincto contra potentiam. Et ista qualitas est subjectum illius visionis secundae quae vocatur apparitio quae est in absentia sensibilis extra, et ipso non existente.—Rep. II, 17, M.

[67] Et praeter istas qualitates est in visu actus videndi qui est subjective in potentia, ut distinguitur contra organuum.—*Ibid.*

Whether as a result of this perceptive act in the external senses there can be habit-formation, is a question that may be asked here. But the answer must await a description of the internal sense perception because of the fact that they form one organic whole. Before describing the act itself, Ockham notes the occurrence in the internal senses, or imagination, of an effect similar to the first noted in the external senses. It is the stimulating or weakening action of the object on these powers. In both cases it is described as not being of the same nature as the object.[68]

The perceptive act is the next phenomenon to be considered in the imagination. Ockham inquires first into the cause or causes of this act. He rejects the suggestion that the object be a direct cause, and the reason alleged is the following. If the object, which is cause of the awareness in the external senses, were also cause of the perceptive act of the internal senses, then the two functions would have to be in operation simultaneously every time the object is present. But this is obviously false since the imagination can operate even in the absence of every object.[69]

He further rejects as possible cause of the perceptive act of the imagination the stimulating or weakening effect referred to above. Nor does he see any permanent effect left by the object in the external senses which could cause this act.[70]

The direct causes of the internal sense cognitive act are, according to Ockham, the sensation or act of awareness itself in the external senses, on the one hand, and the central sense potency, or form, on the other, together with the co-operating first cause, namely God. These three factors are the immediate causes. The causality of the

---

[68] . . . una (*qualitas*) impressa ab objecto, confortativa vel debilitativa, illa est alterius rationis ab objecto extra, sicut illa in visu.—*Ib.* N.

[69] Si dicas . . . a quo causatur primus actus phantasiandi . . . (*respondeo*) non ab objecto sensibili quia tunc phantasia esset in actu suo quando sensus extra esset in actu suo . . . quod videtur falsum.—*Ibid.*

[70] . . . nec ab illa qualitate debilitativa vel conservativa, quia illa per te non est objectum alicuius actus, tum quia illa simul imprimitur cum actu phantasiandi; nec in absentia sensibilis remanet aliquid in sensu exeriori particulari vel communi quod possit cum potentia phantastica primum actum phantasiandi causare.—*Rep.* II, 17, N.

object is only indirect ("causa causae"), seeing that it is a cause of the external sense cognitive act.[71]

Following the description of the cognitive acts of the external and the internal senses, comes the question of the role of habit in each. First, is there to be habit-formation in both or only in one? If only in one, in which?

Ockham uses as criterion the rules governing habit in intuitive and abstractive cognition which we have outlined in the section on the intellect. According to these there is no habit where there is only intuitive cognition,[72] though there are habits wherever abstractive cognition is possible. So the above question about habit can be formulated: is there intuitive cognition in both the external and internal senses, or only in one; is there abstractive cognition in both or only in one?

The cognitive act of the external senses, as described above according to Ockham, has all the characteristics of intuitive knowledge. Therefore it is not surprising to see him classify it as such. It is the medium of contact of the senses with the outside world. Through it, and only through it, can the imagination or internal senses gain their knowledge of this same world.[73]

But along with the intuitive cognition in the external senses is there also the abstractive, which is considered a requisite for the formation of habit? Ockham answers this question with a statement which at the same time provides a solution to the problem of the type of knowledge in the internal senses. It is based on the principle of the organic unity between the two domains of sense cognition. Since there is only one sensitive form and one sense cognitive potency, he argues, why should one duplicate the processes of cognition

---

[71] Respondeo, una causa partialis est visio corporalis et alia est potentia phantastica. Istae duae sufficienter causant cum Deo primum actum phantasiandi; et objectum sensibile extra non est causa illius actus sed tantum est causa causae.—*Ib.* O.

[72] Page 21.

[73] Nunc autem per propositionem frequenter acceptam quando aliquid sic se habet quod illo posito potest aliud poni naturaliter, et illo non posito non potest aliud poni naturaliter, illud est causa illius. Sed sic est de cognitione intuitiva sensus et primo actu phantasiandi, et non de objecto sensibili in actu phantasiandi. Ergo cognitio intuitiva sensus est causa partialis respectu primi actus phantasiandi, et non sensibile extra.—Rep. II, 17, O.

and postulate two abstractive and two intuitive, since there seems to be no necessity for it? It is sufficient, he concludes, that there be only intuitive cognition in the external senses and only abstractive in the internal senses. This is certainly one of the most typical examples of that principle of economy in theorizations known as Ockham's razor.[74]

The question of habit in sense cognition can now be answered. There is only one source of habit in it, and that is the abstractive cognition in the internal senses or imagination. There is no cognitive habit in the external senses.

Habit in the imagination is caused by the initial act (prima abstractive) of this faculty. It tends to reproduce, in the absence of the object of the original intuitive act, knowledge-acts similar to that act.[75]

The cognitive act revived by habit has the same content as the initial act which preceded the habit. Ockham says that both terminate in the one numerically identical object. The same man whom I once saw in reality I can now see in my imagination. It is wrong to say, continues the Venerabilis Inceptor, that the act of imagination terminates in a sort of image of the real person or thing. In fact there are as many distinct acts as there are individuals cognized. He rejects the possibility of having only one mental image for all the individuals of a species. Sense cognition is indeed knowledge of the singular. It would follow from this that Ockham postulates a habit for each singular known through the senses. This habit would explain recurrence in the imagination of the images of

---

[74] . . . pluralitas non est ponenda sine necessitate. Sed non apparet necessitas ponendi talem cognitionem intuitivam in phantasia. Ideo dico quod prima eius cognitio est abstractiva, quia in una forma quae est principium multarum cognitionum sufficit una cognitio intuitiva respectu unius objecti unius potentiae illius formae . . .

Sed alia pars eiusdem formae elicit intuitivam, et illa una intuitiva in una forma circa unum objectum est illa qua iudicatur res esse vel non esse, non mediante abstractiva, cuiusmodi est omnis actus phantasiae sensus et omnium sensuum interiorum.

Sic ergo patet de sensibus interioribus et exterioribus, quid est ponendum in eis et quid non.—Rep. II, 17, T.

[75] . . . qualitas secunda . . . est habitus generatus per actum phantasiandi, inclinans sicut causa partialis ad actus consimiles in absentia rei sensibilis.— *Ib.* N.

individual things seen or heard in the past. And as there is not only
one image for one thing in all the different places in which it has
been seen, but as many as there were separate occasions, it seems
reasonable to conclude that Ockham would admit a different habit
for each distinct occasion in which a person or thing was seen or
heard. Of course not all perceptions leave an equally deep impression. Thus it is explained how some are forgotten and how others
are more vividly recorded.[76]

Habit, therefore, by retaining and reproducing sense impressions, fulfills the function, ascribed by some Medieval writers to an
element called the *species*. For Ockham it is superfluous to postulate
the *species* as a factor in sense cognition. Besides being superfluous,
Ockham contends, the species-theory cannot be said to have been
clearly proposed by Aristotle. In fact, he says, it is not easy to
grasp what the Stagirite meant by *species*: "magna est equivocatio de
specie." Sometimes it refers to acts, sometimes to habits, and sometimes to individuals having the same nature, in which case it can
be said to refer to the form or specific nature (species).[77]

Whether the function of recall performed by habit in the
imagination can be called memory depends on one's definition of
memory. Certainly in a broad sense, says Ockham, one can speak
of memory in sense cognition, for in it exists the power of reproducing knowledge which is similar to that experienced in the initial
perceptive contact with reality.[78]

---

[76] . . . post primum actum, si ipsum sensibile destruatur, potest potentia
phantastica cum illo habitu generato ex primo actu elicere actum phantasiandi
terminatum ad idem sensibile numero quod prius vidi, sicut cognitio
abstractiva intellectus terminatur ad idem singulare numero quod vidi intuitive
in intellectu, et non terminatur ad aliquem similitudinem vel imaginationem,
sicut imaginantur aliqui et false . . .

Eundem enim hominem, quem vidi prius, nunc imaginor . . .

Et secundum illud patet quot sunt individua phantastica, sive sint eiusdem
speciei sive alterius, tot habet phantasma, et sic commune dictum est falsum
quod species habet tantum unum phantasma, quia tot sunt phantasmata quot
sunt individua.—Rep. II, 17, N.

[77] Ad Auctoritatem dico quod magna est equivocatio de specie, quia
aliquando Philosophus accipit speciem pro actu, aliquando pro habitu, aliquando
pro individuo eiusdem rationis, quod potest dici forma vel species.—*Ib*. R.

Omnia illa quae possunt salvari per speciem possunt salvari per habitum.
Ergo habitus requiritur et species superfluit.—Rep. II, 14-15, R.

[78] Primo modo accipiendo memoriam, dico quod memoria reperitur in

However taking memory in the strict sense of recognizing a past act as such, one cannot with certainty attribute it to the senses or the imagination. The reason Ockham gives for this is that these faculties are incapable of reflexive acts, which he considers to be at the root of memory in the true sense.[79]

A review of the main features of sense cognition and the role of habit in it cannot but emphasize the closely-knit character of Ockham's theoretic structure. The external senses enjoy direct contact with the material world through intuitive cognition. The internal senses or imagination depend on the perceptive act of the external senses. Abstractive cognition on the sense level is an exclusive feature of the internal senses. Habit stems only from the abstractive form of cognition. Therefore, there is habit-formation only in the internal senses and not in the external. In a broad sense habit's function in sense cognition can be qualified as memory. However, memory considered strictly as recall of past experiences recognized as such cannot be attributed to habit on the sense level.

A brief summary covering the whole field of cognitive experience will serve as a conclusion to this chapter. It contains two main sections: the first dealing with intellective cognition and the other with sense knowledge. In the former we described the origin of existential knowledge in intuitive cognition, the origin of non-existential knowledge in abstractive cognition and its ability to originate habits, the different factors involved in the process of memory and habit's function in each, and the deterioration of habits in forgetting. In the latter we noted that Ockham attributed intuitive cognition only to the external senses and abstractive only to the imagination or internal senses. The internal alone was said to be capable of habit-formation. The function of habit in sense cognition can be qualified as remembering only in a broad sense of the word.

---

parte sensitiva et intellectiva, quia certum est quod in utraque dereliquitur aliqua qualitas, mediante qua potest in aliquem actum in quem prius non potuit et in actum similem primo actui.—Rep. IV, 12, J.

[79] Secundo modo loquendi de memoria dico tamquam certum quod est in parte intellectiva, sed non ita certum quod est in potentia sensitiva.

Secundum istum modum ponendi potest salvari quod sensus non est reflexivus, quia si potest habere actum recordativum, potest tunc se reflectere super actum suum.—*Ibid.*

CHAPTER III

HABIT IN THE CONATIVE PROCESSES

Grouped together in this chapter under the heading of conative processes are all those non-cognitive experiences which have an overtone of feeling, pleasure, strain, effort, etc. Ockham's analysis of these elements is penetrating and his utilization of the habit-theory to explain some of them interesting.

I. ON THE SENSE LEVEL

Man's composite nature is not only reflected in the duality of his cognitive experiences but also in that of his conative processes. Ockham posits two distinct, though not unarticulated, spheres of conative activity and experience: the sense realm and the intellective, or volitive, realm.[1]

For greater fidelity to the text of the Master we shall begin this discussion with the description of conative experiences on the sense level.

1. IN THE APPETITE

The conative factor to be considered first because it is prior to all the others, including conative habits, is the one known as the appetite. Its priority is one of genetic causality with regards to these, and not one of perceptibility on the part of the observer. In fact, it is not directly observable, since as was noted above, only acts are considered by Ockham as observable psychic phenomena.[2] Appetite is taken here to mean a power or potency of the substantial form

---

[1] Quod autem in homine sunt plures formae substantiales bene est difficile probare vel eius oppositum. Tamen ad praesens probatur sic, saltem de intellectiva et sensitiva, quae sunt distinctae in homine, quia in eodem subjecto non sunt actus contrarii . . .

Ergo istae formae quarum sunt appetitus distinguuntur.—Rep. IV, 7, F.—Cf. Rep. II, 22, H., Quodl. I, 10.

[2] *Ante* p. 4.

and, as such, a subjective source of activity and a partial cause of a total conative experience: "Alio modo (potentia potest accipi) praecise pro illo quod se tenet a parte animae (*sensitivae*) elicientis tamquam principium partiale."[3]

This definition of the appetite becomes clearer when one recalls that, according to Ockham, the potencies are not distinct entities in the form or soul. They are neither distinct from the form nor distinct from each other.[4]

The concept, however, of appetite is different from that of the form and from that of any other potency. Ockham would call it a connotative concept, meaning that it represents one thing directly— the form, and another indirectly or obliquely—acts known as appetitive acts. A clear expression of this view is found in a text where Ockham discussed this characteristic of appetite on the intellective level. That it also applies to appetite on the sense level is quite obvious.[5]

The acts obliquely signified by the concept and term *appetite* and which serve to characterize it will be described in the succeeding sections of this chapter. The reality primarily signified by it is the form itself viewed as cause of the acts. Both the acts and the form or potency concur in the production of habits when these exist. They are said by Ockham to exist when certain tangible or experiential criteria are present.[6] And as these criteria make their appearance, or do not make it, after certain acts are posited, the study of habit on the sense appetitive level is linked up with the study of the different acts attributable to the sense appetite.

2. CONNECTED WITH THE PASSIONS

The term *acts* in the preceding paragraphs was taken in a broad sense and was meant to include all observable phenomena of a conative nature as distinct from the non-observable causal factors

---

[3] Rep. II, 26, d.

[4] Secundo modo non distinguuntur (*potentiae*) realiter sicut res et essentiae distinctae, nec inter se nec ab anima sensitiva.—Rep. II, 26, D.

[5] . . . intellectus et voluntas non differunt secundum istam viam nisi quia intellectus connotat actum intelligendi, et voluntas connotat actum volendi; sed essentia animae non connotat aliquem actum.—Rep. IV, 2, K.

[6] *Ante* p. 4.

like appetite and habit. In this broad sense it includes those appetitive experiences known as passions.

Passions are defined by Ockham as accidental qualities or accidental forms of the appetitive potency, depending for their existence on the presence of cognitive acts on the same level of experience.[7]

Passions can be divided into two main groups. The first, which Ockham considers to be passions in the proper acceptation, includes the experiences identifiable as the acts themselves of the appetite. In this case, the appetite is viewed as an active potency, and acts have the usually accepted narrower sense of the effects of an active power. Included under this heading are such acts as are characterized by their intenseness and vehemence, either in themselves or in the impulse to overt action which is produced. These may be referred to as passions in the strictest sense.[8]

The second group of passions represents an improper use of the term, according to Ockham. These refer to the pleasureable or unpleasant (delectatio vel tristia) effect which can follow from the acts of the appetite which are passions properly so called.[9]

One of the basic differences between these two types of passions is, as we shall see, pertinent to the study of habit. Thus a separate examination of each is required. For greater clarity we shall term the first type *primary* passions and the second *secondary*.

Primary Passions

These experiences are actively produced by the appetite, as by a partial cause at least. That is the significance of the definition of primary passions, according to which they were identified with the

---

[7] Breviter, passio est forma aliqua distincta a cognitione, existens subjective in potentia appetitiva, requirens cognitionem actualem ad suum esse existere.—Quodl. II, 17.

[8] Sciendum tamen quod passio tripliciter sumitur, uno modo proprie, et sic accipitur pro ipso actu elicito a potentia sensitiva.

Primo modo accipiendo passionem potest adhuc capi large, et sic accipitur pro omni actu appetitus sensitivi. Alio modo accipitur stricte, et sic accipitur pro actu intenso et vehemente et vehementer impellente ad actum exteriorem.—Rep. III, 11, H.

[9] Alio modo accipitur passio pro delectatione vel tristita consequente passionem primo modo dicta, et sic accipere est improprie accipere.—*Ibid.*

acts of the appetite. For arguments in favor of this identification, Ockham refers to Aristotle. The Greek Philosopher is quoted as positing only three distinct factors in the *anima*,[10] which the Venerabilis Inceptor here considers equivalent to *form*, that is, sensible form, since he admits passions distinct from these in the intellective form, or soul. These three factors are quoted as being: passions, potencies, and habits. But passions are either the pleasure-pain reactions described above or something that precedes them. And Aristotle does say that the pleasure-pain reactions follow passions.[11] Therefore, Ockham concludes, the primary passions are synonymous with acts, and the above list of factors in the form could be made to read: acts, potencies, and habits.[12]

An objection to Ockham's view representing primary passions as identical with acts of the sensitive appetite is worth considering, because his refutation throws a sidelight on the difference between a psychological distinction and a semantic or grammatical distinction. Thus *anger* and *be angry* are certainly not identical, viewed grammatically. The first represents passivity, according to Ockham, and the second activity. But this opposition results from the possibility of using words in divers functions in sentences; it is a purely grammatical distinction. The objective reality which both refer to is one and the same, namely, the psychological entity we have called a primary passion. Similar examples given by Ockham are *hate* and *to hate*, *concupiscentia* and *concupiscere*. Thus the identity of primary passions and acts of the sensitive appetite is maintained.[13] [14]

---

[10] Nic. Eth. II, 5, 1105b, 20.

[11] Op. Cit. II, 3, 1104b, 14.

[12] Ideo dico cum Philosopho quod in anima non sunt tamen nisi passiones, potentiae, et habitus, et quod ipsae passiones sunt ipsimet actus partis sensitivae. Et per passiones Philosophus intelligit actum. Quod probatur, quia omnis passio vel est delectatio vel tristitia vel aliquid praevium alteri eorum. Sed non est delectatio vel tristitia. Nam secundum Philosophum delectatio et tristitia consequuntur passionem. Igitur passio proprie est actus, et sic intelligit Philosophus. Nec est differentia inter actum et passionem, proprie loquendo.— Rep. III, 11, G.—Cf. Quodl. II, 15.

[13] . . . per exempla, ira enim ponitur passio et irasci actus appetitus sensitivi, et non videtur quod ira et irasci in aliquo distinguuntur. Similiter secundum Philosophum odium est passio partis sensitivi; et tamen ibi non est ponere duplex odium, unum passionem et aliud actum. Similiter est de concupiscentia, quod non est duplex concupiscentia, una actus et alia passio. —Rep. II. M.

[14] Cf. Nic. Eth. II, 5, 1105b, 21.

By identifying passions in the sensitive appetite with the acts of this same appetite, Ockham paved the way for an easy application of his principles governing habit-formation. Every time there is an act-passion, there is the possibility of a habit being formed. And indeed this was the opinion he held during the period of his career in which he prepared his *Commentary* on the Sentences. How this view was later corrected will be seen a little later.[15]

On the strength of his earlier conviction that habit-formation was possible on the sense level as a result of these act-passions, Ockham had determined the possible causes of these reactions. The act-passions were considered immediately dependent on the sensitive appetite as on one partial cause and on a sense cognitive act as on the other. This function of the appetite was described in the preceding section. The participation of the cognitive act in its production requires some consideration. First, Ockham emphasized the point that the act-passion was linked directly with the cognitive act and not with the external object. The meaning of this conclusion is clear. If the object were the direct cause of the act-passion then all persons would be affected in the same manner in a given situation, whereas the contrary is true. Different people are diversely affected by identical circumstances. Still it is true they are affected according to the manner in which these circumstances are cognized.

A second point was also maintained consistently with reference to this earlier view about act-passions and habits. This was that the abstractive cognitive act was capable of participating in their production. And as abstractive cognition on the sense level is an exclusive prerogative of the imagination or internal senses, this assertion can be repeated with reference to this power or faculty.

The third point to be considered presents some difficulties. The question is whether intuitive cognitive acts can also contribute to the production of act-passions and therefore to habits, which is tantamount to asking whether the external senses can contribute. It seems that Ockham wavered a bit about the answer to this query. We find first an affirmative answer, in which causality is attributed to both

---

[15] Et ille primus actus appetitus vocatur passio, et est generativus habitus in tali appetitu.—*Ib.* H. *Cf.* p. 57.

the abstractive and the intuitive, that is, to the internal and external senses.[16]

Only a few paragraphs farther on in the same work, [17] we find this position reversed and the ability of intuitive cognition to contribute to the production of act-passions expressly denied. His argument here is based ort data of observation. In the imagination or internal senses there is evidence to show that there is habit-formation and consequently that there can exist the prerequisite act-passions. A definite inclination favourable to the reproduction of the internal cognitive acts is experienced after the initial acts have been placed. This is true, according to Ockham, of all the types of internal of cognition. Therefore he postulates habit and act-passions in the sensitive appetite as a result of internal sense cognition.

But in the external senses no such inclination is experienced, that is, after an object has been intuitively known by any of the external senses no urge is felt to cognize this object in a manner different from the first time: " . . . alias apprehensum quam primo." In formulating this view, Ockham probably had in mind his parallel discussion of cognitive habits in the external senses. This would explain the use of the word *alias,* for it is also the key-word in his arguments against the existence of cognitive habits here. Since the presence of the object is always required for knowledge in the external senses, no habit seems warranted. No appetitive habit is warranted, Ockham seems to say, since there is no *urge* to cognize differently than with the participation of the object present. This view that act-passions and appetitive habits are produced by the internal senses only seems to have been maintained until the question of the very existence of habit in the sense appetite was re-examined.[18]

---

[16] . . . actus causatur effective ab apprehensione sive cognitione sensitiva, sive abstractiva sive intuitiva, sicut causa partiali una et a potentia appetitiva sicut ab alia causa partiali . . . Et tunc ipsa apprehensio vel cognitio sensitiva, sive sit intuitiva sive sit abstractiva, erit causa efficiens partialis principalis respectu illius actus eliciti ab appetitu sensitivo, et non sensibile extra. Et ille primus actus appetitus vocatur passio, et est generativus habitus in tali appetitu, praedicto modo.—Rep. III, 11, H.

[17] Questio 11 of Book Three of the Commentary contains both opinions, as is attested by not only the Lyons Edition but by the three Manuscripts available to us in photostat, namely: Ob, F, Ma.

[18] Si quaeras cuius sensus appetitus est generativus illorum habitum, respondeo: fantasiae et sensus interioris, et non exterioris . . . Nam apprehenso

The dependence of the act-passions and their corresponding habits on actual abstractive knowledge is not such however that it permits of no exceptions. Ockham visualizes a situation where no such knowledge exists but where the act-passions and the habits seem to exist nevertheless. This is the case of a child born without the use of any external sense and continuing thus. Obviously that child will come to feel hunger and thirst, and therefore desire food and drink. Still the experience of hunger cannot be attributed to any sense perception, either of the external or the internal senses. That there is no external sense perception is assumed in the case, and that there is no internal sense cognition of food or drink can be deduced from the principle of the dependence of the latter on the former. Apart from this hypothetical case, however, actual abstractive knowledge usually is a prerequisite for a primary passion and the beginning of habit-formation in the sense appetite.[19]

The re-examination of the question of appetitive habits on the sense level referred to above is found in the *Quodlibeta* which is probably one of Ockham's latest non-polemic works.[20]

There we see Ockham asking this question: whether virtuous habits can be said to reside in anything other than the will?[21] He

---

objecto per fantasiam et elicito actu appetendi frequenter in appetitu sequente fantasiam, sive objectum existat sive non, sive sit praesens sive non, magis inclinatur talis appetitus ad actum consimilem quam ante actum; per quem in appetitu consequente fantasiam oportet ponere talem habitum generatum ex actibus. Et hoc circa objectum cuiuslibet sensus quatenus fantasiatur.

Sed ex hoc quod aliquis semel appetit aliquod visibile apprehensum a visu non sentit se magis inclinatum ad appetendum illud visibile alias apprehensum quam primo apprehensum, sicut quilibet experitur in se. Ideo in tali appetitu non generatur qualitas sive habitus ex actibus, et sicut non in uno ita nec in alio.—Rep. III, 11, M.

Et ex hoc apparet quod actus appetitus sensitivi causatur mediante cognitione sensitiva abstractiva, non intuitiva.—*Ib.* N.

[19] Si autem non necessario praesupponit cognitionem, tunc causatur totaliter a potentia appetitiva et aliquibus qualitatibus corporalibus. Exemplum: si enim puer natus maneat sine usu cuiuscumque sensus exterioris, iste ut videtur esuriet et sitiet, et per consequens appetit cibum et potum. Tamen iste appetitus non praesupponit aliam cognitionem, quia non in sensu exteriori per casum, nec in fantasia quia fantasia non habet aliquem actum nisi circa prius sensatum.—*Ibid.*

[20] Philotheus Boehner, *The Tractatus De Successivis*, p. 21.

[21] "Utrum in aliquo alio quam in voluntate sint habitus virtuosi?"—Quodl. II, 16.

discusses at length the question of these habits in the sense appetite.
His point of departure however is not different from that of previous discussions of habit in this appetite. He still maintains that some
power or ability is experienced in the sense appetite after repetition
of acts of the will which did not exist there before. For confirmation
of this he refers to the reader's personal experience. Then he adds
for further evidence the case of a virtuous person who has become
demented and lost the use of his free will. Ockham claims such a
person will continue to place acts to which he had become accustomed while enjoying his full mental powers. This he could not do
if there were no residual effect in the sense appetite as a result of
virtuous acts of the will, but quite distinct from the habits of the
will. The question of the nature of this residual effect is not however
immediately decided in favour of the existence of habit, as was the
case in his earlier works.[22] Ockham's later thinking is more empirical
in its approach.[23]

The question is asked pointedly: what is this residual effect
which remains outside the will? First, Ockham points out, it is not
clearly proven that it resides subjectively in the appetitive potency
or for that matter, in the sensitive form itself. On the other hand, it
seems sufficiently evident that it is nothing more than a quality or
quantitative factor in the body. The proof for this contention is
based on observation of the effects of medical treatment. This, Ockham maintains, can produce results similar to those caused by virtuous acts on the part of the will. In other words, the residual inclination to virtue which is not in the will itself but brought about by
the acts of will is not different from that which can be produced by
medical treatment or other artificial means. The Venerabilis Inceptor
credits medical science with the ability to restrain concupiscence and
thus produce effects favourable to the practice of chastity.[24]

---

[22] *Cf.* Rep. III, 10, d.—*Ib.* e.—Summ. Phys. III, 19.

[23] Secundam conclusionem probo quia quilibet post frequentiam actuum
in appetitu sensitivo experitur se magis inclinatum ad consimiles actus quam
ante. Ergo oportet quod aliquod sit in illo appetitu quod prius non fuit; vel
saltem extra voluntatem oportet aliquid ponere. Item ponamus quod sit aliquis
primo exercitatus in actibus virtutibus, sed postea careat usu rationis et fiat
furiosus vel stultus. Manifeste patet quod talis inclinatur ad consimiles actus
quos prius exercebat. Sed hoc non potest esse sine habitu derelicto extra
voluntatem vel sine omni alia re derelicta post actus laudabiles.—Quodl. II, 16.

[24] Sed dubium est quid sit quod manet post tales actus. Dico quod non

In addition, the restraining effect on concupiscence can also be produced by such natural physiological factors as bodily temperature. The inclinations to vice which have their origin outside of the will can be allayed by the increase or decrease of warmth or cold in the body. When this is done, no act on the part of the sensitive appetite is required.[25]

From these observations Ockham concludes that the residual effect we have been referring to, namely, that which is noticeable in the realm of sense experience after acts of virtue have been produced in the will, does not answer the description of a real habit in the sense appetite. The inclination which results from acts of the sensitive appetite is therefore not immediately produced by these acts, as would a habit, but only indirectly. Thus, it is not the acts of craving for food or drink, even repeated, which cause directly the aroused concupiscence but rather the physiological conditions brought about by the assimilation of food and the increased bodily temperature resulting therefrom.[26]

Thus, in one group of circumstances the existence of habit in the sensitive appetite is definitely denied by Ockham. On the basis of his conclusions regarding habits in these circumstances, namely, where the virtue of temperance and the restraining of concupiscence are concerned, he reviewed his entire position on the

---

potest sufficienter probari quod sit aliquod ens existens in appetitu sensitivo, saltem quantum ad multos actus virtuosos, quia potest poni sufficienter quod sit aliqua quantitas vel qualitas corporalis quae inclinant ad tales actus. Quod probo sic. Illud quod potest induci sine omni actu appetitus sensitivi non est ponendum subjective in appetitu sensitivo. Sed omne quod possumus experiri in nobis potest esse in nobis sine actu appetitus sensitivi; ergo etc. Maior est nota. Minor probatur, quia omnis talis inclinatio potest induci per artem medicinae et per alias vias. Nam medici per artem medicinae dirimunt concupiscentiam, et sic disponunt ad actus castos.—*Ibid.*

[25] Patet etiam quod tales inclinationes auferuntur per transmutationem corporalem, puta per generationem vel corruptionem caloris vel frigoris, sine omni appetitu sensitivo vel actu appetitus sensitivi.—*Ibid.*

[26] Et ideo dico quod ex actibus appetitus sensitivi nullus habitus generatur immediate subjective existens in appetito sensitivo, quamvis ex actibus apprehensivis multi habitus immediate generentur; nec post multos actus appetitivos experitur se quis magis inclinatum ad consimiles actus immediate per habitus, sed solum mediate, puta quando appetit comedere et bibere, tunc post comestionem alicuius calidi experitur se magis inclinatum ad actus concupiscentiae quam ante actus appetendi.—*Ibid.*

existence of appetitive habits on the sense level. He admitted that to gather evidence relating to all the other virtues and their residual effects on the sense level would be a big undertaking, and as it had not been done one could not make a general statement covering them all. However, he felt that there was no more reason to postulate a sense appetitive habit in the case of any other virtue of the will than for temperance. Indeed, Ockham goes so far, in concluding this re-examination, as to say that he saw no reason to postulate such a habit under any circumstances.[27]

This negative stand with regard to habits in the sense appetite is adhered to throughout the Quodlibeta[28] which, as we remarked above, is one of the latest of his non-polemic works.[29] It represents a definite break with the position maintained in the Commentary as outlined in the first part of this section. But it cannot be said that the break was not foreshadowed. The reader will recall how Ockham's explanation of forgetting[30] and destruction of intellective habits, generally, is very much akin to this description of the influence of bodily conditions on the practice of temperance. In both cases the residual element on the sense level as a result of acts in the intellective realm was considered a physical or physiological factor. The destruction of this factor could be effected in either case by physical or physiological causes, and its destruction was detrimental to the habits in the will or intellect.

In the preceding paragraphs our attention was centered on passions according to the strict Ockhamistic definition, which we have termed primary passions. The inability of the pleasure-pain reactions to qualify as passions in this strict acceptation does not mean they do not present features equally interesting to the psychologist. The following pages will, we hope, make this clear.

---

[27] Illud totum maxime habet veritatem in virtute temperantiae et in actibus eius, quia isti actus suscitantur et impediuntur per transmutationem corporalem, puta per comestionem vel abstinentiam.

Utrum autem consimiliter sit de aliis virtutibus et quommodo est ibi non est modo dicendum propter prolixitatem. Credo tamen quod eodem modo est in aliis virtutibus. Nec video aliquam necessitatem ponendi quemcumque habitum generatum immediate ex actibus appetitivis inclinantem ad consimiles actus.—*Ibid.*

[28] Cf. Quodl. II, 17; *Ib.* III, 17.

[29] *Ante* p. 55.

[30] *Ante* p. 41.

Secondary Passions

The term *secondary passions* is used here to designate those appetitive experiences on the sense level which Ockham describes as passions in an improper sense. According to Aristotle, it is said, they cannot be called true passions because they are referred to as something which follows passions: "Accipitur passio improprie pro delectatione vel tristitia consequente passionem primo modo dicta."[31] Whether this definition of the pleasure-pain reactions, as we have been calling them, is acceptable to Ockham as their true definition remains to be seen.

A secondary passion is said to be a quality of the sense appetite. As such it is at best passively received in the sensitive form, but it is not necessary, according to Ockham, to attribute positive or efficient causality to the appetite with respect to this experience.[32]

If the appetite is a passive receiver of the secondary passion, then there can be no question of positing a prior act-passion on the part of the same appetite as a cause of the secondary passion. The sole active causes which Ockham would recognize in the production of the pleasure-pain reactions would be the sense cognitive act and the first cause, God. The external object could not be considered an immediate cause.[33]

The sensations of pleasantness or unpleasantness are produced directly by sense cognition. Ockham emphasizes this point by showing that no intermediary act-passion, relating to the same object, is ever present in the appetite at the same time as these sensations. When there exists an act-passion relating to the same object, then that object is viewed as absent. Such is the case for instance when an object is desired or shunned. These feelings are really act-passions, but the object being absent it cannot simultaneously, says Ockham, arouse pleasure or displeasure in the feeling subject, because accord-

---

[31] Cf. *Ante* p. 51, n. 8.

[32] Circa dolores et delectationes et tristitias sciendum est primo quod dolor (*vel delectatio*) qui proprie est . . . qualitas appetitus sensitivi . . . Si tamen appetitus habeat aliquam efficientiam respectu illius passionis, hoc non videtur necessarium ponere.—Rep. (Quaestio Varia) III, 14, B.

[33] . . . dolor (*vel delectatio*) . . . ab apprehensione sensitiva causatur et non ab objecto apprehenso sensu, nec ab actu appetitus, sed solummodo ab apprehensione et potentia appetitiva (*saltem passive*) et Deo.—*Ibid.*

ing to him these are never aroused except by an object which is present. On the other hand, act-passions relating to other objects can exist simultaneously in the sense appetite with pleasure-pain reactions. In this case there is obviously no question of a causal relation between the two types of sensations. Thus Ockham maintains the point that the sense cognitive act is the only immediate, active cause of the secondary passions, barring, of course, the necessary concurrence of the universal first cause, God.[34]

If the sensitive appetite is entirely passive in its relations with secondary passions, as Ockham suggests as more probable, then his denial of the possibility of habit-formation as a result of these reactions seems a foregone conclusion. In the genesis of habit he consistently maintains that the appetite is an active participant, as was explained in our exposition of the principles governing habit-formation.

In addition, the non-existence of habit in the sense appetite as a result of the secondary passions can be deduced from their dependence on an actually existing cognitive act of an object actually present. If after the first instance of a particular type of pleasure-pain reaction there had been habit-formation, then one could expect subsequent recurrences of this experience to be less dependent on the cognition and the object's presence. But this does not seem to be the case.

It would seem that Ockham took the non-existence of habit in the sense appetite as a result of pleasure-pain experiences so much for granted that he did not stop to discuss it. Regarding the same question in the higher realm of the intellective appetite, or will,

---

[34] Tamen appetitus sensitivus non habet simul actus distinctos a dolore sensus et delectationis, sed isti actus immediate sequuntur apprehensionem sensitivam, quia nec per experientiam nec per rationem potest probari quod sit ibi talis multitudo actuum.

Si aliqui actus simul essent cum istis illi essent actus fugiendi, desiderandi, quia alii non apparent in appetitu sensitivo nisi delectationis et doloris. Sed isti non manent cum eis, quia illud est generaliter verum quod dolor sensus et delectatio numquam sunt respectu rei absentis, sed respectu rei praesentialiter habitae. Actus autem desiderandi et fugiendi in appetitu sensitivo sunt semper respectu absentium. Ergo isti actus non manent simul cum dolore et delectatione sensus respectu eiusdem objecti, licet forte possit respectu diversorum.—Quodl. IV, 5.—Cf. Rep. III, 14, B.

where some doubt seemed to have been possible, he does make a clear statement. It may be quoted here in the form of an *a fortiori* argument since in the will, as we shall see later, the secondary passion is preceded by a primary passion, and because of this one would have some reason to expect habit-formation. Still, even there Ockham does not postulate a habit for the secondary passion distinct from that of the primary.[35]

This negative answer to the question of habit connected with pleasure-pain reactions seems to have been consistently upheld by Ockham throughout his entire career. However, this does not preclude the possibility of remembering any particular pleasant or unpleasant sensation of the sense appetite. Ockham did not exclude these experiences as possible objects of recall by memory. On the contrary, he included all past experiences of the intellect, the will, the sense cognitive, and the sense appetitive powers. "Partiale (*objectum*) est actus recordantis praeteritus, et potest esse intuitivus vel abstractivus in intellectu, vel in potentia sensitiva, vel in voluntate, vel in appetitu sensitivo."[36] As a condition for remembering, Ockham postulates, it will be recalled, an initial reflexive cognizance of the sensation when it is actually present. The habit caused by this reflexive act assures the possibility of retention and recall with respect both to the content and the element of past time.

Passions, both primary and secondary, which we have examined may be said to be the most important observable data of consciousness of the conative type on the sense level. There are, however, other elements which must not go unnoticed in a study of this nature. These are commonly known as inclinations resulting from acquired habits. Their characteristic features and exact relationship with habits will be the object of the following section.

---

[35] Ad aliud quod innuitur dico quod delectatio potest esse sine omni habitu. Unde si primus actus ex quo generatur habitus potest esse delectabilis, et ita si semper eliceretur sine habitu posset esse delectabilis, et ita propter delectationem (*vel tristitiam*) non oportet ponere habitum talem.—Ord. I, D. 17, q. 2, G.

Ad aliud dico quod non ponitur habitus propter delectationem plus quam propter tristitiam.—Rep. III, 4, T.—*Cf.* Rep. III, 2, H.

[36] Rep. IV, 12, h.—*Cf. Ante* p. 36, n. 51.

3. THE INCLINATIONS OF HABIT

Our description of the primary passions and of their relations with habit on the sense level revealed that Ockham had serious doubts concerning the necessity of postulating sense appetitive habits during the period of his career when the *Quodlibeta* were composed, whereas in his *Commentary* he clearly admitted their existence. The question may be asked, how does this change of opinion with regard to habit affect his views with respect to the psychological reactions referred to as the inclinations of habits. In other words, do these inclinations stand and fall with the habits?

The answer to this question hinges on the possibility of drawing a clear distinction between what to Ockham's mind was fact of observation and what was theory in this segment of his psychological system. The theoretic factors are by their very nature liable to change, whereas the data of observation remain unchanged. They are the *given*, the constant elements. But are the inclinations facts or theories. according to Ockham?

An indication of what his answer to this question is may be found in his suggestion concerning the possibility of empirically recognizing that there is a distinction between a habit and its inclinations, granted there is a habit. He proposes the case of a man so engrossed in speculative considerations that he does not notice a highly delectable object near him. When, however, he does take notice of it, he feels a strong inclination for it. It is assumed for the purposes of the argument that there is a habit which is ultimately responsible for the inclination. But it must have existed prior to the actual cognizance of the delectable object; still it did not make its presence felt. Therefore, Ockham concludes, the inclination must be something added to the habit as such.

It is apparent from this that the Venerabilis Inceptor considers the inclinations described here to be data of experience. The argument which induced him to conclude from these data to the necessity of habit in his earlier works can be outlined as follows. The sense appetite which affords the basic drive for this inclination is by definition indifferent to any particular object. To explain this well-determined drive or inclination for one object to the exclusion of others, an auxiliary power must be postulated, and this is called habit.[37]

Another, and clearer, indication that Ockham considers the inclination to be the observable fact is his insistence on qualifying the inclinations as acts. Acts, according to Ockham, are the only subjective elements which are directly observable.[38]

It is apparent, therefore, that the inclination is the observable element, and that the habit is the theoretical, explanatory factor.[39] Habit, when it was admitted, was considered to be the sufficient cause of the inclination, which of course existed independently of any imposed explanation. Whether it was to be considered the sole cause of the inclination produced some doubt in Ockham's mind. He proposed it as a possible solution, but immediately added that a better answer would be to consider it one of three partial causes. These three would be: habit, the cognitive act, and the sense appetite.[40]

---

[37] Nam habitus appetitus sensitivo dicit inclinare appetitum, quia appetitus, quantum est de se, potest in plures actus; sed habitus inclinat tantum in unum, puta habitus generatus in parte sensitiva ex actibus luxuriosis inclinativis ad actus consimiles, licet ipse appetitus potest in actum castitatis quantum est de se, et ista inclinatio addit aliquod supra habitum. Patet quia si aliquis primo sit occupatus circa aliquod speculabile, ita quod non apprehendat aliquod objectum concupiscibile et post apprehendat aliquod tale objectum sensibiliter, vel intellectualiter, vel utroque, vel solum sensibiliter, ponatur hoc; tunc experitur quod habet aliquam inclinationem ad illud objectum quam prius non habuit. Sed omnem habitum quem nunc habet in appetitu prius habuit; igitur aliquid novum est in appetitu iam inclinanto quod prius non fuit.—Rep. III, 4, M.

[38] Igitur aliquid novum est in appetitu iam inclinato quod prius non fuit, licet huiusmodi non potest esse nisi actus. Igitur inclinatio illius habitus est actus elicitus.—Rep. III, 4, M.

Ad quaestionem dico quod inclinatio formae (*habitus*) importat quandam activitatem vel quemdam nisum, sive conatum, sine quo potest esse forma. Hoc non potest esse nisi actus. Ideo dico quod inclinatio distinguitur a forma (*habitus*). Quodl. III, 19.

. . . Notitia intuitiva . . . est respectu actuum et non respectu habituum.—Ord. Prol. I, XX.

[39] *Cf. Ante* p. 4, n. 8.

[40] Igitur inclinatio illius habitus est actus elicitus, et respectu huius potest poni habitus totalis causa . . . vel partialis causa cum apprehensione et appetitu, quod magis videtur verum, quia numquam sic inclinat habitus nisi facta apprehensione, quae necessario praecedit omnem actum appetitus.—Rep. III, 4, M.

We are now in a position to answer the initial question of this section, namely, how does Ockham's change of view on the existence of sense appetitive habits affect his views on these inclinations. The answer is that it does not affect them at all. Whatever the explanatory theory, the facts of observation remain the same. Whereas in the earlier explanation the inclinations were said to be the result of habits, in the later they are considered the result or effect of physiological conditions.[41]

In our study of conative factors on the sense level we have passed in review the appetite, the passions, both primary and secondary, and lastly the inclinations acquired as a result of certain acts. The relations of habit to each of these were explored. Now we turn to the field of the intellective appetite.

II. ON THE VOLITIVE LEVEL

As has been frequently noted, the intellective, or volitive, level forms a distinct segment of human experience, according to Ockham. It is an integrated unit, paralleling the sense level, different from it, though not unarticulated with it. The conative experiences on this higher level stem from a distinctive appetitive potency, namely, the will. This faculty is not, however, really distinct from the intellective form, or soul. The term *will*, or *intellective appetite*, represents the soul as being the source of conative activity. Observable experiences referable to the will are listed as: acts, passions, and inclinations. A description of each of these and their relations with habit-formation will throw additional light on Ockham's theory.

1. ACTS, PASSIONS, AND HABITS

Acts and *passions*, viewed as terms, can be considered as having opposing connotations. One implies activeness on the part of the originative source and the other passivity. But whether the psycholo-

---

[41] Minor probatur, quia omnis talis inclinatio potest induci per artem medicinae et per alias vias.

Puta, quando appetit comedere et bibere, tunc post comestionem alicuius calidi experitur se magis inclinatum ad actus concupiscentiae quam ante actus appetendi.—Quodl. II, 16.

gical realities they stand for are distinct and of contradictory natures is another question.

A passion is defined as a certain accidental form, distinct from cognition, existing subjectively in the appetitive potency and requiring for its existence the actual presence of a cognitive act. "Passio est forma aliqua, distincta a cognitione, existens subjective in potentia appetitiva, requirens cognitionem actualem ad suum esse existere."[42] On the other hand, Ockham admits that no act of the will is possible unless some object is presented to it by a cognitive act. "Voluntas non potest aliquid velle nisi cognitum."[43]

The list of passions in the will includes first such experiences as love, hope, fear, joy, etc. Secondly, it is extended to include those we have called secondary passions: pleasure and unpleasantness, "delectatio et tristitia."[44]

There are passions in the will which are not really distinct from acts of the will. Such are those listed first, namely love, hope, etc. These are really acts, directly elicited by the will or by a habit with the co-operation of the will.[45]

Those passions, however, which are referred to as secondary passions, that is, the pleasure-pain reactions, are distinct from the acts of the will. The proof of this, according to Ockham, lies in the fact that the acts can be posited and can subsist in the will without there being any accompanying pleasure or pain. He proposes an example drawn from theology, namely, the case of the devil, who obviously loves himself, yet derives no pleasure from it.[46]

Although the pleasure-pain reactions in the will are distinct

---

[42] Quodl. II, 17.

[43] Quodl. III, 17.

[44] Circa secundum articulum dico primo quod passiones sunt in voluntate, quia amor et spes, timor et gaudium sunt in voluntate. Quae tamen communiter ponuntur, delectatio et tristita etiam sunt in voluntate.—Quodl. II, 17.

[45] Secundo dico quod quaedam passiones voluntatis non distinguuntur ab actibus, et quaedam distinguuntur. Amor enim et spes non distinguuntur ab actibus. Patet per inseparabilitatem ab actibus, sed sunt actus immediate eliciti a voluntate et habitu voluntatis.—*Ibid.*

[46] Sed delectatio et tristitia distinguuntur ab actibus; quod patet ex dictis quia actus voluntatis possunt remanere sine delectatione et tristitia, sicut patet de demone qui necessario diligit se, et tamen in hoc nullo modo delectatur.—*Ibid.*

from its acts, that is, the primary passions, they cannot exist without them. These secondary passions are both produced and kept in existence by the primary ones. They are truly passions and not acts.[47]

The difference between the secondary and the primary passions, also called act-passions of the will, is still more marked when one considers their respective influence on habit-formation. The secondary are capable of no habit-formation. In this they resemble their counterpart on the sense level.[48]

Whether the primary passions, namely those identical with acts, can produce habits in the will is a question which posed a serious problem for Ockham. Though he never denied the existence of habits in the will, he rejected several arguments allegedly proving this point.

The first argument rejected is one drawn from the indeterminate nature or freedom of the will. From this it cannot be concluded that the will needs habit to be inclined sufficiently to a particular act to be able to elicit that act. The truth of the matter is, says Ockham, that the will is just as free and indeterminate, that is, able to choose between a good and a bad action after the second and third act as after the first of any particular kind. In other words, the Venerabilis Inceptor would say that this *a priori* reasoning in favour of habit is contradicted by experience.[49]

---

[47] Sed delectatio et tristitia non possunt esse sine actibus naturaliter, quia ab illis causantur et conservantur. Ergo istae formae sunt passiones non actus.—Quodl. II, 17.

[48] Ad aliud quod innuitur dico quod delectatio potest esse sine omni habitu.—Ord. I, D. 17, Q. 2, G.

Ad aliud dico quod non ponitur habitus propter delectationem plus quam propter tristitiam.—Rep. III, 4, T.

De ratione habitus non est plus inclinare delectabiliter quam tristabiliter. —Rep. III, 2, H.

[49] Non per primum (*probatur, i.e. per indeterminationem vel libertatem voluntatis*) quia quando arguit sic quod voluntas potest elicere actum malum et bonum, ita quod ad neutrum determinetur, igitur indiget habitum determinantem: non valet.

Quia sicut voluntas potest elicere primum actum suum propter libertatem suam bene et male, et propter finem laudabilem et vituperabilem sine omni habitu primo, quia ante actum primum voluntatis non est habitus in voluntate, ita potest elicere actum secundum, tertium, et quartum, et sic deinceps.—Rep. III, 10, G.

Secondly, Ockham denies that the argument for which habit is postulated in the intellect holds for the will. According to him there is habit in the intellect because, once an object has been cognized, the intellect can reproduce knowledge of that object even when it is no longer present, which of course it could not do before the initial cognizance of the object. In the will, however, there is no such ability. It requires the presence of the object, that is, the representation of the object by the cognitive act, not only for the initial act but for all subsequent acts of the same nature. Therefore, there is no common basis for habit in the intellect and the will.[50]

This objection to habit in the will seems to be the one which had the most weight with Ockham, for it is the only one reproduced in the later work, the *Quodlibeta*. It induced him to admit that it is hard to prove the existence or necessity of habit in the will.[51]

Thirdly, Ockham considers that argument invalid which concludes to the existence of habit in the will from the fact that it experiences greater difficulty in eliciting acts at some times than at others. The cause of the difficulty, he says, may be the passions or the habits of the sense appetite.[52]

In spite of these negative considerations, Ockham sees evidence to show that there is habit-formation in the will. When the influence

---

[50] Nec oportet ponere habitum in voluntate propter similitudinem de intellectu. Oportet ponere habitum in intellectu . . . propter hoc quod intellectus post ostensionem objecti, ipso amoto vel destructo, potest in aliquos actus in quos non potuit ante praesentiam objecti, nec requiritur semper praesentia objecti quando intellectus intelligit . . .

Sed voluntas ita indiget ostensionem objecti in tertio vel in quarto actu, et sic deinceps sicut in primo, quia numquam potest actualiter aliquid velle vel nolle nisi actualiter cognitum.—*Ibid.*

[51] Quinto dico quod maior difficultas est de voluntate, quia voluntas non potest aliquid velle nisi cognitum, et actum ita perfectum potest elicere in prima cognitione sicut post multos actus elicitos. Et ideo difficile est probare necessitatem ponendi habitum in voluntate.—Quodl. III, 17.

[52] Nec valet ponere habitum virtuosum in voluntate quia voluntas aliquando difficilius inclinatur ad virtuosum actum quam alias; quia hoc potest accidere propter passiones existentes in parte sensitiva et habitus existentes ibi.—Rep. III, 10, G.

of extraneous factors, such as the sense passions, is kept constant, the sole repetition of acts of the will produces a certain facility to act or an inclination to posit these same acts. In other words, all things being equal ("ceteris paribus"), the sole repetition of acts of the will results in acts of greater perfection and intensity. For this reason Ockham is induced to postulate habits in the will.[53]

The example Ockham gives to illustrate this point is worth considering, not only for its intrinsic value but also because it clearly foreshadows the technique of controlled observation, so widely used in modern laboratory work. He takes the case of a person who is chaste but who has strong inclinations to incontinence. The existence of these inclinations can be assumed since the person under consideration was habitually unchaste up to the present time. Therefore, the element of sensual inclinations is the same now as when the person did not resist their allurements. But a noticeable change is felt now that the person does resist by positive acts of the will. This change is a tendency or inclination to continue the practice of virtue. It must result, Ockham argues, from the only varying element in the case, namely, the acts of the will. Therefore, there are habits in the will, resulting from its repeated acts.[54]

This positive argument for the existence of habit in the will, which is found in the *Commentary* of Ockham, recurs in the *Quodlibeta*. In this later work it is essentially the same but drawn up more clearly. Three observable factors are listed as militating for the existence of habit. These are: greater facility to act, greater inclination or urge to act, and greater difficulty to counteract a set

---

[53] Ideo dico quod virtus (*vel habitus*) est ponenda in voluntate propter maiorem perfectionem actus, et maiorem facilitatem et inclinationem ad eliciendum actus, ceteris paribus, et tunc potest sic argui.

Quaecumque potentia, ceteris paribus, magis inclinatur post actum quam ante et ad intensiorem actum, et ex illis acquirit habitum. Sed voluntas est huiusmodi, quia omnibus paribus existentibus in parte sensitiva, magis inclinatur ad actum nunc quam prius.—Rep. III, 10, G.

[54] Patet de continente qui habet pravas concupiscentias et non sequitur eas, et tamen prius sequebatur eas. Non est hic aliqua variatio in parte sensitiva, quia ita posteriores concupiscentiae sunt pravae sicut primae. Nunc autem voluntas prona et inclinata est ad non sequendum eas, et prius non, aliter non esset continens. Ideo ibi videtur quod sit aliquis habitus necessario ponenda. Item non magis est habitus negandus in voluntate respectu unius objecti quam respectu alterius.—*Ibid.*

pattern of action. These are said to exist as a result of acts of the will, since all the other contributory factors, as for instance those originating in the sense processes, are kept constant. In presenting this argument, Ockham makes no exaggerated claims for its value. He uses such terms as: "one can reasonably hold, or be persuaded, etc."[55]

Ockham's stand on the question of habit in the will remains unchanged throughout his works. Though he admits the existence of habit, he is cautious in his choice of arguments. All primary passions, that is, those identical with acts are capable of producing habits. The secondary passions, that is, the pleasure-pain reactions do not cause any. Indirectly though, as a result of reflexive cognizance, they can be preserved in memory just as any subjective act can.

2. INCLINATIONS OF HABIT

The observable factors listed above as militating for the existence of habit in the will may be reduced to these two: facility to act and an inclination to act. Of these two, the former receives little attention from Ockham apart from a brief statement in the *Commentary*. There it is said that, were it for the facility alone, habit would not need to be considered an active element. Furthermore, it is said that the facility seems to flow from the inclination to act. Whether this can be construed to mean that Ockham would not consider the facility to act a directly observable element is a question we shall not decide. In any case, he states clearly that the inclination is the primary reason for postulating habit, and the facility a secondary reason.[56] [57]

---

[55] Potest tamen teneri rationabiliter et persuaderi; tum quia facilius post executionem potest voluntas elicere multos actus quam antea, ceteris paribus in parte sensitiva; tum quia post multas dilectiones voluntas magis inclinatur ad diligendum; tum quia post multos actus elicitos circa aliquod objectum cum maiori difficultate et tristitia potest elicere actum contrarium quam ante omnem actum, sicut quilibet experitur in se. Ergo necesse est ponere habitum generatum ex illis actibus.—Quodl. III, 17.

[56] Ad aliud dico quod (*habitus*) non requiritur propter facilitatem vel promptitudinem tamquam principium activum tantum. Sed propter inclinationem dicitur proprie principium activum; et ex hoc sequitur facilitatio et promptitudo quia magis inclinatur nunc quam prius, et ita principaliter ponitur propter inclinationem, secundario autem propter alia duo.—Rep. III, 4, U.

[57] *Promptitudo*, which does not appear in other pertinent passages, is used here, we believe, as a synonym of *facilitas*.

Though the element of facilitation of acts by habit is not given any particular consideration, the inclination is given careful study. This latter, viewed on the sense level, it will be recalled,[58] was termed an act itself. By calling it an act Ockham solves the problem of its direct observability, since acts are observable and habits are not. But can an inclination of the will be called an act without opposition from theologians? He admits there is a problem involved.[59]

The theologians' position can briefly be stated thus: granted that a person who had previously been afflicted with a vicious habit receives the grace of God, obviously that person cannot remain in the state of grace while committing mortal sins. Therefore, if the inclinations of the subsisting habit are themselves acts, and we assume for the sake of the argument acts of grave import, then the inclinations cannot exist in the soul while it is in the state of grace. Yet Ockham maintains that it is a matter of experience that the inclinations of the habit can be felt by a person presumably in that state. Thus, he suggests the example of a person who perceives an object which was connected with his previously acquired habit. Immediately he feels an urge or inclination not only in his sense faculties but also in his will. The drive in the will can indeed become so strong that resistence to it and acting in a manner calculated to preserve the grace of God become well nigh impossible. How can Ockham as a theologian reconcile his view that inclinations are acts with the admitted fact that the inclinations of a bad habit can remain in the soul which is in the state of grace?[60]

---

[58] *Cf. Ante* p. 63.

[59] Et eodem modo est dicendum de habitu in appetitu sensitivo et intellectu . . . Inclinatio illius habitus est actus elicitus . . . Sed de voluntate est maior difficultas.—Rep. III, 4, M.

[60] Posito quod aliquis primo habeat habitum viciosum, acquisitum ex actibus viciosis, et tamen sibi post subito infunditur gratia. Tunc est dubium utrum stante gratia in voluntate potest aliquis actus elici secundum inclinationem habitus viciosi. Videtur quod non quia nullus potest peccare mortaliter dum est in gratia. Sed habitus ille inclinat ad actum peccati mortalis, igitur, etc.

Sed oppositum experitur quilibet in se quantumcumque sic presentetur sibi ·objectum illius habitus viciosi, puta aliquid concupiscibile, hic experitur quod non tantum habet actum in appetitu sensitivo sed in voluntate. Et maiorem inclinationem habet in voluntate quam habuit ante apprehensionem

He reiterates the opinion that the inclinations are really acts and explains that as such they are caused concurrently by the will and the habit.[61]

To solve the problem, however, he introduces the notion of an act of will which is caused by it but not freely. For most acts the will is free. There is no doubt about that, according to him. But for this act, synonymous with inclination, the will is not free. It is described as an act before an act. Thus Ockham hoped to be in agreement with the general opinion of the "doctores" who held that the inclinations were natural reactions for which man was not responsible: "primus motus." They involved neither merit nor demerit.[62]

Though Ockham emphasizes the distinction that must be made between inclinations originating in the will itself, as for instance the inclinations of habit, on the one hand, and inclinations felt by the will but originating on the sense level on the other, he does not mean to belittle the latter. Their importance, not only as psychological factors but also as moral determinants, cannot be denied.

3. INCLINATIONS IN THE WILL FROM THE SENSE APPETITE

In pointing out the distinction, according to Ockham, between the two levels of experience in man, we have more than once remarked that he does not consider the two spheres of activity unarticulated. An instance of how the two are related is provided by the

---

intellectualem illius objecti, quia aliquando habet tantam inclinationem in voluntate quod vix potest resistere et elicere actum oppositum ad quem inclinat gratia, etc.—Rep. III, 4, M.

[61] Huiusmodi autem inclinatio non potest esse nisi actus elicitus ab habitu, quod credo esse verum . . . potest dici quod ille actus causetur partialiter ab habitu et partialiter a voluntate.—*Ibid.*

[62] Sed tunc stat difficultas quommodo in illo actu non consistat peccatum, cum eliciatur a voluntate. Potest dici quod licet voluntas sit libera respectu cuiuslibet actus ab eo eliciti absoluti considerati; tamen considerando aliquem actum voluntatis inquantum ille actus antecedit in voluntate non est voluntas libera respectu illius actus . . .

Tunc dico quod non est in potestate voluntatis quando eliciat .cum habitu inclinante aliquem actum circa illud, et ille actus potest dici primus motus qui excusatur a peccato secundum doctores . . . Ideo nec in eo consistit meritum nec demeritum.—Rep. III, 4, N, O.

influence on the will of sense conative experiences. This influence
is great enough to deserve the qualification of partial causality with
respect to some acts of the will. Therefore, to the list of possible
contributory causes of these acts, namely, the will itself, habit, the
object, and the cognitive act, Ockham adds the acts of the sense
appetite.[63]

To be more specific with regard to the sensitive acts, considered
partial causes of the acts of the will, it must be stated that the term
sensitive acts is taken very broadly here and includes sensitive
passions, both primary and secondary. In fact Ockham seems to
attribute this causal influence more particularly to the secondary
passions. It is the pleasure or pain felt in the sensitive appetite which
is viewed as a determinant of the act of the will. Thus, a pleasant
sensation resulting from a certain act of the will can be considered
a contributory cause of that act; and a foreseen unpleasant one a
deterrent from an act which would produce it.[64]

The extent of this causal influence of the sense reactions on the
will is, however, never such that it necessitates or determines the
will's act completely. The will is always free to consent to these inclinations or to oppose them. But they can be so vehement that they
render this very difficult.[65]

Indirectly however, the inclinations of the sense appetite can

---

[63] Ad primum istorum dico quod non est generaliter verum quod omne
inclinans ad actum est potentia, objectum, vel habitus. Nam cognitio actualis
in intellectu quodammodo inclinat voluntatem ut causa partialis sui actus.
Actus appetitus sensitivi inclinat quodammodo voluntatem sicut causa partialis.
—Rep. III, 2, J.

[64] Secundo dico quod potest reddi aliqua causa quare causatur actus volendi
respectu objecti, quod causat delectationem in appetitu sensitivo, et actus
nolendi respectu objecti, quod causat dolorem in eodem; quia potest dicere
quod actus appetitus sensitivi, sive melius ipsa delectatio in appetitu sensitivo
est causa effectiva partialis immediate concurrens cum voluntate et cognitione
talis objecti ad causandum volitionem. Et similiter dolor est causa effective
partialis ad causandum actum nolendi respectu talis objecti.—Rep. (Quaest.
Var.) III, 14, U.

[65] Ad aliud dico quod habitus et passiones proprie loquendo non inclinat
voluntatem nisi quando consentit eis mediante volitione. Et ita si voluntas
nolit illas passiones et nolit elicere actum secundum habitum non inclinabunt
voluntatem . . . Et ista est inclinatio quam homo difficulter vincit, quia cum
difficultate potest non consentire talibus passionibus.—Quodl. III, 22.

become completely overwhelming for the will. They can blind and obstruct the reasoning powers, by impeding the operations of sound judgment. Without the guidance of these, the will is morally helpless. Therefore, the influence of sense on the higher powers can be devastating.[66]

The precise nature of the influence of these inclinations on the will, notwithstanding his efforts at explanation, presents a serious problem according to Ockham. Just why the will is sometimes inclined more and sometimes less, or why, in the face of strong pressure from the senses or against an imperative dictate from the intelligence or other outside influences, it still maintains its basic freedom is not explained. It can choose to act in accordance with these solicitations; it can choose to act against them; or it can choose not to act at all. Beyond recognizing the fact itself, little can be said about it but that it is a natural feature of the will. As a process it lies beyond the scope of our observation.[67]

Albeit that the inclinations of sense do not impair the basic freedom of the will, they can cause great distress in the will when it counteracts them. There is, however, a means of alleviating this distress, says Ockham quoting Scotus.[68] This consists in presenting to the will something that is more delectable to it than the sensate experience. It is as if, by this means, the will were provided with a lever to pry itself loose from the attachment to the sensate delectation.[69]

---

[66] Praeterea appetitus sensitivus potest impedire iudicium. Sic quando aliquae passiones possunt esse ita vehementes in appetitu sensitivo quod totaliter impediant iudicium rationis.—Rep. III, 12, QQ.

[67] Sed istis non obstantibus, non redditur causa quare voluntas plus vel minus inclinatur, positis talibus passionibus in appetitu sensitivo; quia quantumcumque ponatur delectatio vehemens in sensu et cognitio dictativa in intellectu et alia concurrente ad actum, adhuc est in potestate voluntatis elicere actum volendi respectu illius objecti vel nolendi, vel nullum actum elicere. Et ideo respectu illius inclinationis voluntatis non videtur posse reddi aliqua causa nisi quia natura rei talis est, et hoc innotescit nobis per experientiam.—Rep. (Quaest. Var.) III, 13, U.

[68] *Cf.* Op. Ox. III, d. 25, q. 2 (Vives XV, 82.)

[69] Et dicit hic Johannes quod voluntas non videtur seipsam retrahere posse sine difficultate quando condelectet appetitui sensitivo. Et ideo ad delectabiliter retrahendum se oportet aliquid delectabilius causari in eo quam sit delectatio appetitus sensitivi quo finis (*objectum voluntatis*) sit sibi delectabilior.—Rep. III, II, J.

With regard to the deeper contentment in the will, by means of which the attractions of sense are overcome, Ockham quotes Scotus[70] as saying that it must be supernatural in origin. According to Ockham, the Subtle Doctor considers certain inclinations of the sense appetite to be more potent than any natural delectation, presumably in the will. For this reason Scotus postulated the necessity of a supernaturally-produced feeling in the will to outweigh it.

The Venerabilis Inceptor argues in favour of the sufficiency of naturally-produced feelings in the will to counteract the pleasures of sense. Psychologically speaking, he explains, an act of the will produced by supernatural help is not different from one produced by natural powers alone. This does not mean he contends that all acts, producible with supernatural aid, are also under any circumstances producible naturally. Rather, all acts, once produced naturally or supernaturally, are the same from a psychological standpoint. Therefore, the delectable effect produced by one is no different from that of the other. In other words, he would say that loving God with the help of grace, though this alone is meritorious, produces no greater palpable happiness in the soul than loving Him with the forces of nature alone. Therefore, if the attractions of sense can be overcome by a superior contentment in the will, this feeling can be caused by natural forces alone as well as with the help of grace.[71]

The illustrations given by Ockham may serve to clarify the issue. An unbaptized person, he contends, brought up in christian surroundings and educated in the Faith can believe in God naturally and elicit all the acts, psychologically speaking, pertaining to the Faith. He is able to love God. From this love of God can spring such happiness that no sense delectation is too great for it to overcome.[72]

---

[70] *loc. cit.*

[71] Et dicit hic Johannes . . . illud autem non potest fieri per aliquod naturale, quia illa delectatio in appetitu excedit omnem delectationem naturalem; igitur per aliquid supernaturale. Contra: ista delectatio habita mediante habitu supernaturali non habetur nisi mediante actu. Sed actus elicitus circa Deum mediante tali habitu est eiusdem rationis cum actu elicito sine eo ex puris naturalibus. Ergo eodem modo delectatio consequitur actum mediante habitu naturaliter acquisito sicut infuso—Rep. III, 2, J.

[72] Item sicut aliquis nutritus inter christianos credit articulos fidei, ita potest omnes alios actus elicere pertinentes ad fidem, et per consequens potest naturaliter Deum diligere.—*Ibid.*

Aristotle is quoted as saying that the pleasure resulting from speculation is the greatest possible happiness for man.[73] This, Ockham explains, is certainly a naturally-produced happiness. The conclusion implied is that this happiness can counteract the attractions of sense.[74]

Finally, Ockham illustrates his point by comparing the soul's ability to absorb sadness (presumably caused by conflict with sense allurements) with its ability to produce happiness. He states that it can naturally absorb sadness, including, we presume since no reservations are made, the highest degrees of distress. To do this it must be able to produce a counterbalance in the form of happiness. This could result from loving God naturally above all things. Hence, Ockham concludes, there is no sense attraction which, all things being equal, cannot be counteracted by a greater weight of happiness in the will, produced even naturally.[75]

This penetrating analysis of the interactions of the two levels of conative experience in m .n is climaxed by an illuminating, though brief, reference to the role of the supernatural in this mutual relationship. However perfect one may possibly consider the control of the will over the senses to be without grace, it is not supernatural because God does not accept it as such. Absolutely speaking, of course, He could have decreed that this mode of good behaviour be acceptable to Him. But He did not. Thus only such conduct as is performed with the help of grace is supernaturally meritorious. Regarding the effects of original sin, Ockham states that man's natural powers are not sufficient to quash the rebellion of the senses. To have complete rest and tranquillity, with no internal conflict arising from the senses or otherwise, one would need to have the gift of impassibility.[76]

---

[73] *Cf.* Nic. Eth. X, 7, 1177a, 24.

[74] Item delectatio quae est in speculatione est maxima secundum Philosophum. Sed. illa habetur naturaliter; ergo, etc.—Rep. *1b.*

[75] Item aliquis potest mediante habitu et actu acquisito naturaliter absorbere tristitiam. Ergo eodem modo potest mediante habitu naturaliter diligere Deum, et sic habere delectationem. Ideo dico quod illud potest fieri per habitum naturalem sicut per supernaturalem.—*Ibid.*

[76] Si dicas quod tunc ex puris naturalibus aliquis posset vitare omnem pecatum, dico quod non, quia Deus non acceptat illam moderationem per habitum naturalem sicut per supernaturalem. Tamen posset sic acceptare, si sibi placeret.
Ad aliud dico quod rebellio non potest auferri, et perfecta tranquillitas

These pages on the influence of sense appetitive acts on the will revealed Ockham, the psychologist, at his best, it seems to us. Despite his reluctance to theorize on the basic element of human freedom, he attributes causal influence to the inclinations of sense with regard to the will's acts. The will is represented as being able to take delight in the pleasure of the sense appetite. But no such sensible experience can directly despoil the will of its essential liberty. On the contrary, the will is able to derive satisfaction from experiences more consonant with its immaterial nature, and this satisfaction can counter-balance the pleasures of sense. This activity is purely natural, of course, and is not supernaturally meritorious because we are assuming it is accomplished without grace, as it can be. When it is accomplished with the help of grace, then it is supernatural because of God's supernatural order.

Our study of conative experiences on the higher, or volitive, level included first a definition of acts and passions in the will, and their influence on the formation of habits in the will. Secondly it gave a description of the inclinations resulting from habits in the will. These inclinations, we noted, are acts and therefore directly observable elements, but they are not acts in the complete sense of the word because they do not entail moral responsibility. Thirdly, our study comprised an examination of those inclinations which are felt in the higher sphere of experience but which originate in the lower. Ockham's views on the relations between the two spheres of conative endeavour were analysed at that point.

III. ON THE PHYSICAL LEVEL

Though the realm of physical activity is an integral part of that broader unit of man's psychological constitution described as the sensitive level of experience, its contribution to this unit can be studied apart. Physical actions are viewed by Ockham as originating from the same potency as the sense cognitive and appetitive acts. With respect to these actions this potency, which is not distinct from the sensitive form, is called the executive potency.

---

fieri nisi per aliquid supernaturale infusum, non per aliquid naturale ex causis naturalibus causatum, sed per supernaturale, puta per dotem impassibilitatis.—Rep. III, 2, J.

A physical action is known as an operation of the executive potency. This potency is therefore the principle cause of these operations. Another cause, however, and the one which is probably responsible for the type of action produced, is the passion, or act-passion, of the sense appetite. Thus, when one feels inclined to eat, the feeling is the act-passion, and the action of eating is caused by this feeling in conjunction with the central potency.

The will can also be a causal factor in the production of physical actions. Beyond this statement nothing is said which would help to clarify Ockham's views concerning the immediacy of the will's intervention in physical activity.[77]

The possibility of habit-formation as a result of physical actions was consistently admitted by Ockham, but little descriptive detail concerning the process is given. In the *Commentary*, representing his earlier views, we find a brief statement giving the essential nature of habit as a power which elicits or helps to elicit acts rather than it *terminates* them in the manner of an object of cognition with regard to a cognitive act. Then Ockham gives a few instances of physical habits or skills, namely, those acquired by scribes, and all other artisans or craftsmen.[78]

The only reference to this question in the *Quodlibeta*, which represents Ockham's later thinking, is equally brief, and couched in very much the same terms. There is evidence, he explains, to warrant positing habits in the body. The power that elicits the actions of the body, which he calls the executive potency, shows greater ability to produce these acts after it has performed them a number of times. This added facility, which can be experienced especially by scribes,

---

[77] Tam habitus appetitus sensitivi quam actus qui vocatur passio habet aliqua alia objecta, puta actus potentiae executivae. Exemplum: quando appeto comedere, actus comedendi est objectum tam actus illius quam habitus in appetitu sensitivo . . .

Aliquando autem habitus voluntatis (*et actus*) respiciunt tamquam objecta operationes potentiarum executivarum quarum istae passiones (*sensitivae*) sunt principia efficientia partialia.—Rep. III, 11, M

[78] Ideo dico quod illud derelictum habet magis rationem inclinantis et elicientis partialiter . . . quam terminantis . . . In organo exteriori potest poni talis qualitas inclinans, sicut patet in scriptoribus, in cantoribus, et in omnibus operantibus manualiter.—Rep. II, 17, L.

weavers, and also other artisans, is a positive acquisition, since it can hardly be considered a privation of a previously existing power.[79] This acquired facility and this power are attributed to habit.[80]

There is one more type of physical habit mentioned by Ockham. This does not represent skill in the performance of any action but rather the fixity and automatism which results from always doing things in the same way. Thus, one who has become accustomed to going from one room to another by a door which is in a certain place will find himself inclined to continue this practice even after its location is changed. Ockham considers the action produced by habit in this case to be not only specifically the same as those which caused the habit but even numerically the same. For skills, generally, he would say that the actions resulting from the habit were only specifically the same from one performance to another.[81]

The few brief references made by Ockham to physical habits indicate that he considered them to exist and to be ultimately caused by the sense appetitive potency, called the executive potency in relation to them. Contributory causes are the sense act-passions and the will which can share in the production of the actions which are immediately responsible for the habits or skills.

This chapter has presented Ockham's views on the nature of conative experiences and the role of habit in producing them. It

---

[79] This constitutes Ockham's clearest and most concise formulation of the habit-theory. Hence it was also presented above when general norms and criteria were discussed. See p. 1-2.

[80] Ad quaestionem dico primo, quod necesse est ponere habitum in corpore. Quod patet, quia potentia executiva corporalis per multos actus elicitos potest in consimiles actus in quos non potuit ante, vel saltem non ita faciliter ante tales actus, sicut patet in scriptoribus, textoribus, et in aliis artificibus. Ergo in illis potentiis est aliquid additum vel ablatum. Sed non apparet quod aliquid sit ablatum. Ergo dicendum est quod aliquid sit additum. Illud voco habitum.— Quodl. III, 17.

[81] Et tamen non omnes illae qualitates inclinant tantum ad aliquod eiusdem rationis, sed ad idem individuum numero. Patet in aliquo inclinato ad transeundum per certum ostium et locum et in certa pariete domus. Et post mutetur ostium adhuc frequenter reddit ad locum ubi fuit ostium, quamvis per multos actus generetur qualitas inclinans ad transeundum per secundum ostium. Et ita qualitas inclinans ad transeundum per primum ostium inclinat ad idem individuum numero, non tantum specie.—Rep. II, 17, L.

singled out for consideration first the conative processes on the sense level. In this field Ockham corrected an earlier view admitting the possibility of habit-formation and attributed the effects, once attributed to habit, to physiological factors.

A second section of this chapter studied the conative reactions in the will. There the existence of habit was consistently maintained by the Venerabilis Inceptor. The subject of inclinations of habits in the will was also treated, and a few notes on inclinations experienced in the will but originating on the sense level were added.

The third and last part examined Ockham's teaching on the question of physical habits or skills. It was noted there that the physical actions responsible for these habits were linked causally with acts and passions of the sense appetite. The appetite under the name of executive potency was considered the main drive behind these actions and habits. The influence of the will in this domain was recognized by Ockham but not examined in detail.

In the next chapter it will be shown how man's cognitive and conative experiences are integrated in the pattern of man's moral behaviour from which happiness should result.

CHAPTER IV

In Moral Behaviour

The moral structure of man is viewed here, at least in its abiding elements, as a closely-knit network of habits. This network is woven around an initial link or loop. It is woven according to a certain pattern. In other words, there is a psychological basis for moral habits, both as a starting point and as a growth-process. What this starting point and this process are must now be examined.

I. Subjective Basis of Virtue

The ultimate subjective basis of morality, according to Ockham, is the will. Without the participation of the will, therefore, there can be no moral, or virtuous, acts, and consequently no moral, or virtuous, habits. Only the acts of the will are worthy of praise or blame; only habits derived from these are virtuous or vicious. Aristotle is quoted as saying that only acts which are in our power can be blameworthy.[1] Nobody, it is explained, can be blamed for being blind, unless the blindness is a result of personal sin.[2]

That the concurrence of the will in the eliciting of an act is essential if that act is to be a moral act, is illustrated by Ockham by a comparison with the participation of right reason as a factor in morality. This latter is not the basic element, since an act performed in conformity with right reason by the first cause alone, namely

---

[1] *Cf.* Nic. Eth. III, 1, 1109b, 30.

[2] Quarta, quod solus habit voluntatis est proprie virtus . . . probatur, quia habitus ille proprie est solum virtuosus cuius actus est solum virtuosus. Probatur, quia solus actus voluntatis est laudabilis vel vituperabilis. Igitur solus ille est virtuosus. Igitur habitus generatus ex tali actu est virtuosus solum.

Confirmatur per Philosophum, 3 Ethicorum, ubi dicit quod nullus actus est vituperabilis nisi sit in potestate nostra. Nullus enim culpat caecum-natum, quia est caecus sensu. Sed si sit caecus per peccatum, tunc est vituperabilis.— Rep. III, 10, D; H.

God, would not be meritorious or virtuous. Therefore, the subjection of an act to the will is the all-important factor.[3]

The will is viewed by Ockham as capable of choice (electio) independently of right reason. Thus, granted that choice is essential to morality, this strengthens the will's position as subjective basis of morality. All that is psychologically required for the will to elicit its act is the represented presence of the object in a cognitive act. In this respect it is comparable to the sense appetite. No prior judgment or dictate of reason is required psychologically in either case.[4]

The ultimate subjective condition for an act to be moral is that it be "in the power of the will" ("in potestate voluntatis"). This is true not only for those acts which are referred to as acts of the will, but for all the various acts performed by man. On condition that an act, whatever its specific nature, be dependent on the will, then it can be moral. And only as long as this dependence lasts can it qualify as a potentially moral act. Thus, a physical action can be originated by the will and then reach a stage where it is no longer under the control of the will. As an example of this Ockham suggests the case of a man who throws himself from a precipice willingly but regrets his action in the course of the descent. At the origin this action was definitely bad, but with the change of intention came a change in the moral character of the act. As the person was not able to halt the continued fall, and thus was not responsible for it any longer, there is nothing to prevent this act of repentance from being virtuous and meritorious.[5]

---

[3] Ad aliud dico quod ex hoc quod praecise est conformis rationi rectae non est virtuosus, quia si Deus faceret in voluntate mea actum conformem rationi rectae, voluntate nil agente, non esset ille actus meritorius nec virtuosus. Et ideo requiritur ad bonitatem actus quod sit in potestate voluntatis habentis talem actum.—Rep. III, 10, R.

[4] Item contra hoc quod ponit quod electio in voluntate non potest esse nisi praecedat iudicium rationis, quia non maior ostensio objecti requiritur a parte voluntatis quam a parte sensitivi, sed ad hoc quod appetitus sensitivus habeat actum suum non requiritur nisi sola apprehensio objecti, sine omni iudicio, sicut quilibet experitur. Igitur ad hoc quod voluntas habeat actum suum requiritur ostensio objecti praecedens, sine omni iudicio rationis.—Rep. III, 2, I.

[5] Praeterea, nullus actus est virtuosus nisi sit in potestate voluntatis, quia non est peccatum nisi voluntarium. Sed alius actus ab actu voluntatis

Granted that the morality of human acts stems from their association with acts of the will, does this mean all acts of the will are moral, that is, either good or bad? Or are there even in the will acts that derive their morality from other acts of the will?

In answering these questions, Ockham establishes as a first point that there are at least some acts in the will which are always moral. These do not need to derive their morality from any others. They are moral in themselves, and are called necessarily moral acts. Because of their importance these deserve detailed examination. First, with regard to the term *necessity* as used here, it must be pointed out that there is no question of absolute necessity in moral acts. Ockham sees no absolute necessity in anything which is created. Even our moral acts are contingent. Furthermore, these acts can be performed by God alone and thus be deprived of their morality because of the lack of human participation.[6]

The sense in which necessity can be ascribed to the acts referred to is that of hypothetical necessity. That means they cannot be caused by the will without being moral. Therefore, if and when they are caused by the will, they are moral in view of a divine precept.[7]

Secondly, with regard to the meaning of necessity in moral acts, Ockham points out that, unless some acts of the will are always moral and necessarily so, no basis of morality can be found. If all its acts were contingently virtuous, that is, derived their moral character from some other act, there would then be no such thing as virtue or vice. Therefore, some acts of the will must be moral in

---

primo potest esse in potestate voluntatis et post non, puta si aliquis dimmitat se voluntarie in praecipitium, et post peniteat et habeat actum nolendi illum descensum meritorie propter Deum. Tunc in descendendo non est in potestate voluntatis; ergo ille actus non est necessario viciosus.—Quodl. III, 14.

[6] Circa expositionem affirmativam dico primo quod de virtute sermonis nullus actus est necessario virtuosus. Hoc probatur, tum quia nullus actus necessario est, tum quia quilibet actus potest fieri a solo Deo, et per consequens non est necessario virtuosus quia non est in potestate voluntatis.—Quodl. III, 14.

[7] Tamen aliter potest intelligi actum esse necessario virtuosum, ita quod non potest esse viciosum, stante praecepto divino. Similiter, quod talis actus non potest causari a voluntate creata nisi sit virtuosus, et sic intelligendo dico quod aliquis actus voluntatis est necessario virtuosus.—*Ibid.*

themselves and by themselves. From these, others can then derive their morality. Ockham gives as an example of an act contingently moral, the action of walking. This action can either be moral or not moral. When it is moral, it has derived this morality from some other act. Now if this second act is also contingently moral, then it must acquire its morality from another, and so on indefinitely. Unless some act is necessarily moral, no act is moral.[8]

Not only are acts necessarily moral required by reason, but there actually are some which answer to this definition. Ockham gives as example the act of loving God above all things. Such an act cannot be elicited without it being virtuous, because it will always be in accordance with the expressed will of God which binds men in all places and at all times.[9]

Thus Ockham establishes the first point with regard to the moral character of acts of the will, namely, that there are some which are necessarily moral. The second point he goes on to demonstrate is that not all acts are necessarily moral even in the will. In other words, he defends the possibility of indifferent acts in the will. Such acts, he explains, are indifferent which are posited with reference to objects consonant to the will's normal activity but which lack the conditions required to make them good or bad. Thus, if I were to love someone for a purpose which is neither good nor bad; if my love were neither in accordance with nor against right reason;

---

[8] Quod probo quia impossibile est quod actus contingenter virtuosus, ita quod indifferenter potest virtuosus esse vel viciosus, fiat determinate nisi propter alium actum necessario virtuosum.

Hoc probatur, quia actus contingenter virtuosus, puta actus ambulandi, fiat determinate virtuosus propter conformitatem ad alium actum, quaero de illo actu: aut est necessario virtuosus modo praedicto et habitur propositum quod est aliquis actus in voluntate necessario virtuosus; aut fit determinate virtuosus propter conformitatem ad alium actum virtuosum contingenter, et de illo est quaerendum sicut prius, et erit processus in infinitum, vel stabitur ad aliquem actum necessario virtuosum.—*Ibid.*

[9] Tertio dico quod ille actus necessario virtuosus modo praedicto est actus voluntatis, quia actus quo diligitur Deus super omnia et propter se est huiusmodi. Nam ille actus sic est virtuosus quod non potest esse viciosus, nec potest a voluntate creata creari nisi virtuose. Tum quia quilibet pro tempore et loco obligatur ad diligendum Deum super omnia, et per consequens ille actus non potest esse viciosus, tum quia ille actus est principium omnium actuum bonorum.—Quodl. III, 14.

furthermore, if neither the circumstances of time or place, or any other circumstance affected it morally; then my love would be an indifferent act.[10]

The meaning of indifferent acts is further clarified by Ockham. They are such that they cannot become necessarily moral. Their moral character, when they acquire it, will not be intrinsic. Only those acts are intrinsically moral which primarily deserve praise or blame.[11]

When indifferent acts cease to be indifferent and become morally good or bad it is because of their connection with another act which is moral. Thus the act of love which was described above as indifferent can become good or bad by association with a good or bad intention, or with other circumstances which have a moral character. Ultimately, they derive their morality from acts which are necessarily moral in the sense explained above.[12]

The morality of human conduct originates in the will, therefore. Only acts of the will are intrinsically moral, but not all acts of the will are such. Some are indifferent. These can become moral by being linked with another act which is moral intrinsically.

II. OBJECTIVE NORM OF VIRTUES

If some acts of the will are moral and others are not, it must be concluded that morality is in the will but not *of* or *from* the will.

---

[10] Utrum sit actus aliquis indifferens in voluntate . . . qui potest dici bonus et malus denominatione extrinseca vel neutra . . . Actus ille voluntatis est indifferens qui elicitur circa objectum conveniens tali actui sine tamen circumstantiis requisitis ad bonitatem vel malititam actus, puta si diligam aliquem hominem non propter aliquem finem bonum vel malum, nec secundum rationem nec contra, nec loco nec tempore determinat necnon, et ita de aliis circumstantiis virtuosis vel viciosis, iste actus non esset bonus moraliter nec malus, sed indifferens et neuter.—Rep. III, 10, O.

[11] Respondeo quod idem numero non potest esse indifferens et post intrinsece bonus vel malus. Et dicitur ille actus intrinsece bonus vel malus cui primo convenit laus vel vituperium, et cui primo est imputabilis.—*Ibid.*

[12] Ad hoc igitur quod fiat bonus vel malus oportet eum circumstantiari circumstantiis virtuosis vel viciosis, puta quod voluntas diligat illum hominem propter finem talem et tempore determinato, et sic de aliis. Sed sic diligendo habet actum alium, sicut dictum est prius, ergo et alium actum voluntatis.— *Ibid.*

What then is the ultimate criterion of morality? Is it a quality of
the act itself? Is moral rectitude a perfection of the act, and turpitude
the lack of due perfection? Ockham denies the statement that morality is ultimately a quality of the act. According to him, it is rather a
quality of the will itself; it consists in the perfection of the will which
conforms itself to the true norms of morality, and turpitude is the
lack of this perfection. These objective norms are the precepts of
God. Therefore, those acts of the will are morally good which are
elicited in conformity with these precepts inasmuch as they are known
through right reason.[13]

The divine precepts are norms of morality inasmuch as they are
expressions of the will of God. In the last analysis, therefore ,it is
the will of God that is the root of morality. This does not mean
that man is obliged to will all that God wills, but only that which
He wishes man to will. Thus, it can happen that God's general plan
contradicts the individual injunctions to be fulfilled by man. The
death of Christ, for instance, was willed by God from all eternity.
Yet God did not want the Jews to desire his death in the way they
did.[14]

For the better understanding of this thesis, concerning the will
of God as the absolute and ultimate norm of morality, it may be
useful to examine the illustrations presented by Ockham. Supposing
God, he explains, had forbidden a person to honour his parents,
that person would sin by honouring them, because he would be
disobeying God. Similarly, if God had prescribed that another person honour his, he would sin by not honouring them. This, of course,

---

[13] Dico ergo quod deformitas non est carentia justitiae vel rectitudinis
debitae inesse actui, sed est carentia rectitudinis debitae inesse voluntati;
quod non est aliud dicere nisi quod voluntas obligatur aliquem actum elicere
secundum praeceptum divinum quem non elicit. Et ideo rectitudo actus non
est aliud quam ipse actus quem debuit elici secundum rectam rationem.—
Quodl. III, 15.

[14] Sed tenetur (*voluntas*) se conformare voluntati divinae in circumstantia
objecti voliti, puta quia tenetur velle quod Deus vult eam velle . . .

Ad primum istorum dico quod non semper voluntas est recta quia conforma-
tur voluntati divinae . . . nam aliquando vult Deus aliquid et tamen vult
creaturam nolle illud. Exemplum: Deus ab aeterno voluit mortem Christi,
tamen noluit Judaeos velle mortem eius eo modo quo est mortuus ab eis.—Rep.
(Quaest. Var.) III, 13, O.

is a theoretical supposition and is not meant to refer to any actual situation.[15]

A more practical illustration given by the Venerabilis Inceptor concerns the precept of loving God above all things. It involves a student who is so absorbed in his studies that he has no opportunity to think of God or elicit acts of love of Him. We assume that the studies he is so absorbed in constitute his duty of state. Supposing, then, that he did actually interrupt his studies to elicit an act of love, would this act be meritorious or not? Ockham queries whether the obligation to study can be so specific a precept of God that to interrupt this work would mean an act of disobedience. In that case would the student, by trying to please God, actually offend Him by his disobedience, since to love God above all things means to do His will at all times?[16]

Pushing this principle of morality to its logical extremes, Ockham asks whether God could command a person, such as the student in the present case, not to love Him. Theoretically speaking, answers Ockham, it is possible, since no contradiction is involved; but in practice the will could not do it, for it would still be loving God by obeying even the precept not to love Him.[17]

God's will as a norm of morality can be a norm only inasmuch

---

[15] Et si dicatur voluntas numquam debet esse deformis voluntati divinae, sed iste qui vult honorare parentes quos Deus non vult honorari habet voluntatem deformem voluntati divinae; ergo peccat in honorando. Dicendum est quod si Deus vult eos non honorari nec ab isto nec ab illo, iste peccat in honorando parentes suos. Si tamen Deus non vult eos honorari ab alio, sed vult eos honorari ab isto, iste in honorando non peccat, nec est deformis voluntati divinae, sed est conformis voluntati divinae.—Ord. I, 48, H.

[16] Si dicas quod Deus potest praecipere quod pro aliquo tempore non diligatur Ipse, quia potest praecipere quod intellectus sit sic intentus circa studium vel alium actum et voluntas similiter quod nihil possit pro illo tempore de Deo cogitare. Volo quod voluntas tunc eliciat actum diligendi Deum, tunc ille actus non est virtuosus, quia elicitur contra praeceptum divinum; et sic actus diligendi Deum super omnia non erit virtuosus.—Quodl. III, 14.

[17] *Respondeo*: si Deus posset praecipere sicut videtur sine contradictione, dico tunc quod voluntas non potest pro tunc talem actum elicere, quia ex hoc ipso quod talem actum eliceret Deum diligeret super omnia; et per consequens impleret praeceptum divinum, quia hoc est diligere Deum super omnia diligere quidquid Deus vult diligi.—*Ibid.*

as it is known to man. A human being cannot, of course, be expected to know all the desires of the Divine will. But when a thing is known to be in accordance with the will of God, man is obliged to be submissive with regard to this manifestation of God's will either actually or habitually, according to the nature of the volition.[18]

To God's will in general as the norm of morality and virtue must correspond an habitual readiness to conform to this will. Ockham postulates a moral habit in man to facilitate this habitual readiness. This habit should be possessed by all who have reached the age of reason and therefore have, or are able to have, some notion of God.[19]

The object of this general habit is to dispose the human will favourably towards the accomplishment of God's will as a general norm. It is not considered to be directly linked with acts which are the fulfilment of individual precepts. Remotely however, it is conducive to the placing of these acts. The act of submission which it produces directly is a causal factor in the production of the acts of obedience to particular precepts. The general habit is therefore a "causa causae" with respect to these particular acts.[20]

---

[18] Tertio dico quod non quilibet tenetur se conformare voluntati divinae volendo volitum a Deo habitualiter immediate quia non tenetur scire illud esse volitum a Deo, et per consequens non tenetur velle illud habitualiter immediate. Tamen si sciat illud esse volitum a Deo voluntate beneplaciti tenetur illud velle, hoc est, in illo complacere vel habitualiter vel actualiter.—Ord. I, 48, E.

[19] Et si quaeratur quis est ille habitus qui inclinat ad volendum omnia a Deo volita, dicendum (*est*) quod aliquis talis quo complacet voluntati omne illud quod complacet voluntati divinae; qui debet esse semper in omni habente usum rationis postquam ad aliquem Dei cognitionem attigerit vel potuit attingere.—Ord. I, 48, D.

[20] Iste autem habitus non inclinat immediate ad omne volitum a Deo. Nam oportet praesupponere cognitionem qua sciatur hoc esse volitum a Deo, et mediante illa inclinat ad actum. Potest tamen distingui de mediata inclinatione ad actum. Ut uno modo dicatur mediate inclinans quasi non sufficiens ad inclinandum, et sic habitus praedictus inclinat ad volendum hoc volitum a Deo. Aliter dicitur mediate inclinans quia non concurrit nec sufficit per se nec cum aliquo ad talem actum volendi hoc volitum a Deo. Sed primo inclinat ad aliquem actum qui postea est causa ipsius. Et sic etiam ille habitus inclinat mediate quia primo inclinat ad actum quo complacet voluntati creatae omne quod fit a Deo.—Ord. I, 48, E.

These pages on the moral aspects of habits have shown that a distinction must be drawn between the subjective basis of morality and the objective norms of morality. The latter transcend the former. The will, which is the subjective basis, is imperfect if it does not abide by the objective norms. These are the known manifestations of the will of God. Acts performed in accordance with this will are morally good; acts performed in opposition to it are bad. In addition to man's willingness to carry out the particular injunctions of the Divine will, there must exist an over-all readiness to be submissive to this will at all times. This general disposition is influential, at least remotely, in the accomplishment of the individual tasks imposed by the eternal Legislator.

III. Elements of a Virtuous Act

Since, according to Ockham, the will is the subjective basis of morality, only acts of the will can be intrinsically moral and all other psychological acts, to become moral, must be linked with a moral act of the will. The exact nature of this link will now be examined more closely. The list of psychological acts concerning which the problem of this relation can be posed includes the acts or passions of the sensitive appetite, the dictates of right reason, and even those acts of the will which have reference to the end or purpose of an act. To this list of psychological acts can be added such physical actions which, because of the particular circumstances of time and place in which they were placed, can assume a moral character, when they stand in a specific relation to the will. None of these acts or actions can be sources of morality, strictly speaking. They cannot participate in the causation of the act of the will in which morality primarily resides. Ockham qualifies them all as being objects of the moral act. How he applies this generalization to each factor will be seen by taking up the study of each in particular.[21]

---

21 Ad secundo dico . . . actus ille in appetitu sensitivo, sive passio quae est objectum virtutis commune, sive recta ratio, sive locus sive tempus, sive finis, sive quaecumque circumstantia est objectum partiale actus virtuosi in voluntate. Non est causa efficiens illius actus.—Rep. III, 11, R.

The Dictates of Right Reason

These dictates, according to Ockham, are not the initial judgments formed by the intellect consequent on the apprehension of an object. They consist in the act whereby the intellect assents to, or dissents from, these judgments.[22]

True, the dictates of reason, that is, the assent or dissent, are not required, psychologically speaking, by the will to elicit acts, since it can do this after the initial judgments have been formed in the mind. But from a moral standpoint, for an act of the will to be virtuous, it must in some manner be associated with the dictates. The nature of this association will be described a little later.[23]

Though the dictates of right reason are said by Ockham to be necessary for the accomplishment of a virtuous act of the will, they cannot be said, according to him, to be causes of such an act. The reason he gives involves the distinction between a natural human potency and a voluntary or free one. The former, of which the intellect is an example, are called natural because they are not free; the latter, of which the will is the only example, is free. The will alone can therefore be a source of morality and merit. Right reason cannot render meritorious an act which is not meritorious.[24]

If the contribution of right reason, while being necessary, is not one of causal influence on the moral act, then it can only be of the nature of a necessary condition or constituent element of that act. That is what Ockham means when he calls the dictate of right reason an object of the virtuous act. By calling it an object, he

---

[22] Et sciendum est quod actus dictandi intellectus non est formaliter complexum, sed est actus assentiendi vel dissentiendi complexo iam formato.—Rep. III, 11, X.

[23] Quemcumque actum respectu quorumcumque objectorum aliorum a recta ratione potest voluntas elicere mediante recta ratione, potest elicere sine ea cum sola apprehensione eorum objectorum.—Quodl. III, 15.

[24] Secundum probatur ex primo, quia si per solam positionem actus prudentiae (*rectae rationis*) fieret actus voluntatis virtuosus qui prius non erat virtuosus propter carentiam illius actus, cum actus ille prudentiae sit mere naturalis, et nullo modo in potestate nostra, sequitur quod de actu non virtuoso fieret actus virtuosus et econverso per positionem et destructionem actus mere naturalis qui nullo modo est in potestate nostra, et de non digno vita aeterna fieret dignus vita aeterna per aliquod mere naturale, quod nullo modo est in potestate nostra.—Quodl. III, 15.

associates it so closely with the act of the will that it cannot be changed without affecting the specific nature of the moral act, since the nature of acts is determined by their objects. Thus Ockham retains the important role usually assigned to right reason in the realm of morality.[25]

The End of The Act

The end, or purpose, of an act which is intrinsically virtuous is also viewed as an object of that act. This, according to Ockham, seems obvious from the fact that when something is desired in view of something else, this latter object is considered more desirable than the former. Both are however objects of desire. When the two are presented to the will separately, they can cause two distinct acts of the will. Nevertheless, the act which has reference to the most desired object can be a cause of the act which has reference to the other object. If these two objects, says Ockham, should now be embraced in one single act of desire, the former object would be regarded as the principal object of the act and the other the secondary. In any case, both are simultaneously objects of the moral act. In this manner the Venerabilis Inceptor substantiates his claim that the end of a virtuous act is an object of that act. It is that object for which the other objects are desired or loved.[26]

---

[25] Si autem dicis quod talis actus non est virtuosus propter defectum prudentiae (*actus rectae rationis*), contra (*tenetur*). Pono quod coexistat actus prudentiae, et tunc quaero utrum ille actus voluntatis sit virtuosus vel non. Si non, nulla causa huius potest dari nisi quia recta ratio non erit eius objectum, quia nullum aliud objectum requisitum deficit per casum, et recta ratio coexisti. Si . . . sit virtuosus . . . oportet quod habeat rectam rationem pro objecto.—Quodl. III, 15.

Sed unus alius actus alterius speciei qui haberet rectam rationem pro objecto et non ille.—*Ibid.* Cf. Rep. III, 11, X.

[26] Praeterea probatur quod finis est objectum actus virtuosi, tum quia quando voluntas diligit aliquid propter finem magis diligit finem, tum quia si essent duo actus respectu diversorum objectorum quorum unus esset causa alterius, si illa duo objecta diligerentur unico actu, illud objectum esset primum cuius actus esset causa alterius quando diliguntur distinctis actibus. Sed si quis diligit finem uno actu et illud quod est ad finem alio actu, actus respectu finis esset causa actus illius quod est ad finem. Ergo quando diligo aliquid propter finem unico actu. finis est objectum principale respectu illius actus.—Quodl. III, 15.

Physical Actions

Physical actions, when they form part of a virtuous act, are also termed objects of this act by Ockham. The reason given is that they manifest the characteristics of an object in that by changing them the nature of the act itself is changed. Thus, eating can be a good thing in certain surroundings and at certain times, but in different surroundings and at different times this action can be morally offensive.

With regard to an act which is morally indifferent, the elements of time and place can indeed be no more than circumstances which, when changed, do not affect the nature of the act. Thus, from the point of view of a physical action, like going to church, for instance, not only the elements of time and place, but even the intention for which it is done, and the dictates of reason which may be associated with it, are mere circumstances. They do not affect the basic action of going to church. But when viewed from the angle of an act as a moral act, all these possible determinants of such an act must be considered as objects of the act because by changing any one of them the act may become quite different, morally speaking.[27]

The Passions

Before discussing the association of passions with moral acts of the will as objects of these acts, it must be pointed out that the passions or acts of the sensitive appetite (which alone are under consideration here) have no intrinsic moral character of their own. By themselves they are neither good nor bad. Ockham establishes

---

[27] Idem patet de loco et tempore quod sunt objecta, quia aliter esset actus voluntatis ita perfecte virtuosus sine illis sicut cum illis; quod falsum est, quia velle comedere est actus virtuosus si vult loco et tempore, et aliter est magis viciosus quam virtuosus. Dico ergo breviter quod omnes circumstantiae sunt objecta partialia actus necessario virtuosus.

Sunt autem circumstantiae cuiuscumque actus qui solum dicitur virtuosus per denominationem extrinsecam, per conformitatem ad actum necessario virtuosum, quia quilibet talis actus potest semper idem remanere, circumstantiis variatis, sicut potest esse actus ambulandi ad ecclesiam propter bonum finem et malum, cum recta ratione et contra rectam rationem. Ideo respectu talis actus ista dicuntur circumstantiae. Actus autem intrinsece virtuosus variatur per variationem cuiuscumque circumstantiae, quia variato objecto non potest esse idem actus propter transitum a contradictorio in contradictorium.—Quodl. III. 15.

this by the following argument. If the passions, he says, possessed any intrinsic morality, this would be possible only through their conformity or non-conformity with right reason. But this reason cannot be adduced according to him, since even the operations of the sense organs can be performed in accordance with right reason, and yet no one attributes intrinsic morality to these.[28]

Since passions are morally indifferent, Ockham concludes that, to become morally good or bad, they must be associated with a moral act of the will as objects of this act. They are styled common objects because the same passion can be related to more than one moral act or virtue.[29]

In these pages on the constituent elements of a moral act, we have seen that Ockham defines as the object of such an act elements which have no direct causal effect on the morality of the act but which are so intimately tied up with it that they cannot be changed without changing the specific moral nature of that act. Such possible elements are the dictates of right reason, the end of an act, sensitive passions, and physical actions. Of all these, the sensitive passions give rise to the greatest number of problems in this respect. Hence it will be studied in greater detail.

IV. Moral Significance of Passions

Through Virtues

The sense passions are termed objects of virtuous acts of the will by Ockham, not merely because they can be considered as the fulfilment of the will's appetitive impulses, but also because they can be brought into existence by the will, at least indirectly. Any passion

---

[28] Sed actus quicumque talis (*sensitivus*) non est proprie et intrinsice virtuosus. Hoc probatur quia si hoc sic sit, hoc non esset nisi propter conformitatem ad rectam rationem. Sed hoc non valet . . . quia actus cuiuslibet organi esset proprie virtuosus quia potest conformiter elici rectae rationi . . . Et tamen nullus ponit virtutes in talibus organis.—Rep. III, 10, F.—Cf. *Ib.* H., Quodl. II, 15. Ib. 17.

[29] Secundo, virtus (*et actus voluntatis*) est circa passiones sicut circa materiam quia passiones sunt objecta communia actus et habitus virtuosi essentialiter.—Quodl. IV, 7.

Tam actus intellectus quam voluntatis terminatur ad timores et audacias tamquam ad objecta *communia* istorum actuum (Italics ours).—Rep. III, 11, O.

can be aroused by the will, and can therefore be considered an object in the sense of effect, that is indirect, not only of the acts of the will but also of the virtues corresponding to these acts in the will. A virtuous act concerning a passion entails a double act therefore: first, the immediate act of will, produced by the virtuous habit directly in the will, and second, the act, or passion, of the sense appetite commanded (imperatus) by the act of will.[30]

The will's influence in producing passions is indirect, as was noted. It attains directly the sense apprehension from which the passion results in the appetite. Thus, it is a "causa causae" with respect to the passions. This suffices to justify Ockham's claim that all passions can be commanded by the will, though it is not said that this can be done at any time and under any circumstances. More factors than the will are needed to produce the apprehensive act from which the passion results.[31]

However indirect, this power of the will and of virtue over the passions of the sense appetite has an important bearing on the moral significance of these passions. Man's inner balance depends to a great extent on his being able to arouse passions when they are useful and quell them when they are harmful. To take one example: if a person were so deprived of taste for food as to be unable virtually to eat he would be miserable; on the other hand, if his appetites were so potent that he felt obliged to eat continuously, he would be no better off. Thus happiness and virtue depend on man being able to control his passions, at least, contain them within definite limits.[32]

---

[30] Dico quod quaelibet passio potest esse objectum voluntatis et alicuius virtutis, quia quaelibet potest imperari a voluntate . . . Sic dico ergo quod habitus virtuosus voluntatis habet duplicem actum, unum elicitum ab habitu et aliud actum in appetitu sensitivo qui est objectum habitus sicut est objectum actus eliciti ab habitu.—Quodl. IV, 7.

[31] Est (*voluntas*) causa mediata respectu illarum passionum, quia est causa causae. Est enim causa immediata partialis apprehensionis praecedentis talem actum qui vocatur passio.—Rep. III, 11, M.—Cf. *Ib.* R.

[32] Ad aliud dico quod virtutis est excitare passionem quando oportet et ubi oportet, etc. . . . . Sed virtutis est sedare et refrenare passiones viciosas sive superabundantes sive deficientes, et eas reducere ad medium secundum debitas circumstantias; et tales passiones consistentes in medio virtus habet excitare. Exemplum, ille qui non habet passiones simpliciter est insensibile et viciosus sicut numquam comedens dicitur viciosus, et qui habet passiones superabun-

The effect of virtue on the passions consists, therefore, in
arousing some sometimes and quelling these or others at other
times. Does this mean that one and the same virtue can have contrary effects on the level of the sense appetite? In answering this
question, Ockham recalls that the immediate effect of any virtue,
or virtuous habit, is an act of will. This act of will can embrace as
its object opposing elements on the sense level. It can call forth a
certain degree of fear and a certain degree of daring to cope with
one particular situation. Both are objects of the one act of the will.
This act itself, however, is simple and its nature corresponds to that
of the virtue which elicits it. It can still be referred to as the act of
such a virtue, no matter what particular degree of one passion or
of its opposite is commanded by the act. This is illustrated by Ockham
by a comparison with a similar phenomenon on the cognitive level.
A single act of the intellect can embrace the knowledge of what is to
be feared in some circumstances and dared under other circumstances. So a single act of the will can elicit or command several
opposing elements on the level of sense passions.[33]

To illustrate his explanation of the manner in which contrary
effects on the sense level can result from one individual virtue in the
will, Ockham examines a number of virtues in particular. *Fortitude*
is the first example proposed. This virtue inclines the will to command passions involving fear and daring. But neither of these in
their extreme form is elicited in this instance, says Ockham quoting
Aristotle as authority.[34] The passion which is produced holds a mid-

dantes dicitur viciosus sicut semper comedens. Sed ille qui comedit ubi
oportet, etc. dicitur virtuosus; et sic habet aliquommodo excitare passiones et
aliquommodo sedare et refrenare.—Rep. III, 11, S.

[33] Ad aliud dico quod virtus moralis in voluntate quae est proprie virtus
non inclinat ad actus contrarios tamquam principium effectivum et elicitivum.
Inclinat tamen ad actum qui respicit contraria, sicut objecta partialia et
communia. Et ideo actus voluntatis virtuosus potest terminari ad timores et
audacias quae sunt actus partis sensitivae et non eliciti a virtute in voluntate.

Nam sicut intellectus potest per unum actum formaliter dictare quod est
timendum pro loco et tempore et aliis circumstantiis, et quod est audendum
alio tempore et secundum determinatas circumstantias, ita potest voluntas per
unum actum velle timere et audere cum debitis circumstiis, ita quod tam actus
intellectus quam voluntatis terminantur ad timores et audacias tamquam ad
objecta communia istorum actuum.—Rep. III, 11, O.

[34] *Cf.* Nic. Eth. III, 8, 1117a, 4

dle position with regard to these extremes. It negates both extremes as being opposed to the virtuous act of the will. In this case, the opposing passions are not really present as objects of the act of will, but are connotatively designated by the same term which designates the passion actually present. This is the mean between the two opposing extremes.[35]

Whether the same virtue of fortitude which inclines the will to command the passion which is the mean between fear and daring can also under different circumstances incline the will to command only fear and not daring, or only daring and not fear, is a question left open by Ockham. He states that one could consider these two effects to originate in two different forms or degrees of fortitude, or one could consider them the result of one and the same virtue having the power to produce fear or daring according to the circumstances.[36]

As examples of virtues of the will which have negative effects on the passions, Ockham quotes *temperance* and *continence*. Both, he says, are concerned with base concupiscence, but the former with a milder form of it than the latter. Temperance, which deals with moderate concupiscence, is able to quell this passion completely, and the resulting virtuous act even causes a pleasant feeling in the will, which exceeds the allurement of the passion. Continence has to struggle with a vehement and overwhelming degree of the same

---

[35] Quantum tamen ad modum loquendi Philosophi, dico quod intelligit quod fortitudo inclinat ad aliquem actum voluntatis qui non terminatur ad timores et audacias; sed inclinat ad actum qui terminatur vel imperat actum appetitus sensitivi a quo istae passiones negantur. Et ideo inclinatur ad negationem utriusque actus tam timoris quam audaciae, quia istae passiones sunt extremae et connotant vicium in actu; sed inclinat ad actum partis sensitivae modo praedicto, qui actus non debet dici timor nec audacia sed debet habere denominationem mediam, sicut actus debet esse medius et repugnare extremis.—Rep. III, 11, P.

[36] Alius autem actus fortitudinis vel eiusdem virtutis potest terminare ad timorem secundum circumstantias determinatas puta si recta ratio dictet quod uno tempore sit timendum potest voluntas tam virtuose velle timere, et si dictet quod alio tempore est audendum potest tunc velle audere. Et istae volitiones sunt diversarum fortitudinum, si sint diversi actus quorum unus inclinat virtuose ad timendum et non ad audendum, alius ad audendum et non ad timendum. Et possent esse eiusdem fortitudinis, et idem inclinet ad velle timere uno tempore et velle audere alio tempore.—Rep. III, 11, Q.

type of passion. This it resists, at least to the point of not giving in, but is unable to quell completely. The resulting virtuous act in the will is noticeably feeble and certainly leaves no comfort in the will, if indeed it does not produce a certain amount of sadness.[37]

Sense passions, therefore, have no moral significance in themselves, but derive it from the acts of the will whose function it is to command them to be elicited or to quell those which are undesirable. Both extremes of one type of passion can be related to one single virtue, that is, through the act produced by that virtue in the will. Fortitude is an example of a virtue which is interested in eliciting a positive passion, which can either be the mean between fear and daring or some degree of either according to the circumstances involved. Temperance and continence are example of virtues concerned with quelling existing passions in the sense appetite. Basically, it is the same sort of passion for both, but temperance has to contend with a milder form than continence. The former quells its corresponding passion completely, wheres the latter succeeds merely in maintaining its resistance to the powerful passion it has to deal with.

V. Residual Effects Of Virtues On Passions

In view of the control exercised on the passions by the virtues, the question may be asked whether this effect is merely transitory or can also be of a more permanent nature. In other words, it may be asked whether habits, or something akin to habits, can be formed in the sense appetite as a result of the control by virtues. This does

---

[37] Ad aliud dico quod temperantia et continentia non differunt nisi secundum magis et minus, quia sunt eiusdem speciei . . . Tam temperatus quam continens habet pravas concupiscentias in parte sensitiva, et neuter eas sequitur. Sed differentia est in hoc quia temperantia non habet concupiscentias superabundantes et vehementes nec quasi invincibiles sed remissas. Continens autem habet concupiscentias pravas excellentes et quasi invincibiles, et non sequitur eas sicut nec temperatus.
Alia differentia quia temperatus potest elicere actum virtuosum secundum habitum virtutis, actum inquam intensum et cum magna delectatione in voluntate quae excellit delectationem consequentem concupiscentiam in appetitu sensitivo . . . Sed continens habet concupiscentias superabundantes quas non potest omnino sedare, vel si potest, ille actus elicitur cum modica vel nulla delectatione, quasi cum tristitia, et erit actus remissus valde.—Rep. III, 11, T.

not entail a re-examination of Ockham's final stand against habits in the strict sense of the word in the sense appetite.[38] Irrespective of what theoretical explanation is adopted for certain data of observation, these data cannot be challenged. The question here is whether certain residual or lasting effects can be observed on the sense level as a result of the effects of virtuous conduct. If such exist, we shall term them quasi-habits in view of Ockham's final over-all theoretical evaluation of these observed data. The texts presented, being from the earlier works, do not distinguish between facts and explanations of facts; residual effects are called habits.

In answering our question, Ockham first lays down this negative principle: no residual effect in the passions is absolutely required for the existence of virtues in the will. Granting that the effect of virtues is favourable to the growth of such residual effects or quasi-habits the resistance to this growth on the part of the sense appetite can be so great as to impede it completely. Still virtuous habits can subsist in the will, itself, in spite of this.[39]

Although not necessary, residual effects in the sense appetite are producible as a result of virtues and can serve a useful purpose, according to Ockham. As an example of a case when this happens, he cites the virtue of temperance. One residual effect can be the destruction, that is, the permanent weakening, of the passion opposing this virtue. Another can be the positive inclination to virtue arising from physiological conditions, as was quoted in our discussion on Ockham's reasons[40] for rejecting habits as such on the level of sense appetite.[41]

---

[38] *Cf. Ante* p. 55 ff.

[39] Sit haec prima conclusio, quod nulla virtus moralis necessario coexigit habitum consimilem in parte sensitiva. Hoc patet, quia quantumcumque actus eliciantur in appetitu sensitivo generativi habituum, tamen potest esse tanta rebellio carnis ad spiritum quod causatio talis habitus potest omnino impediri.— Rep. (Quaest. Var.) III, 12, LL.

[40] *Cf. Ante* p. 57 and Quodl. II, 16.

[41] Non videtur inconveniens quod voluntas causet et conservet aliquem habitum in parte sensitiva . . . sicut patet de actibus temperantiae et aliis virtutibus qui requirunt actus in parte sensitiva.—Rep. *Ib.*

Temperatus, secundo modo loquendo, non solum fugit actum nolendi concupiscentias pravas sed occasionem talium, et ideo per actus temperantiae possunt illi actus destrui.—Rep. (Quaest. Var.) III, 15, E.

Residual effects, or quasi-habits, are therefore admitted in the sense appetitive field or in the physiological structure of man as a result of virtues. In addition to this, Ockham states that these effects can remain even after the virtue of the will has been replaced by its corresponding bad habit. Thus the tendency to eat moderately produced on the level of sense as a result of virtue in the will can subsist after the will has lost its virtuous habit of wanting to eat moderately. Even more true is it that certain residual effects on the lower level can persist when virtues other than those which caused these effects have been lost.[42]

Besides clarifying Ockham's position on the question of the possibility of residual effects in the realm of sense as a result of virtues in the will, these last few paragraphs have shown in what relation these two factors stand to each other. It was seen that either can exist without the other, or at least continue to exist, as in the case of the sense factors, when the other no longer exists. But within the same sphere do the several habits or factors depend on each other and to what extent? This problem shall now be taken up.

VI. Integration Of Virtues

The question of the relations between the divers residual effects on the sense level need hardly detain us since Ockham gives it only slight consideration and, apparently, only in his earlier writings, when he still maintained the possibility of habits, as such, in the sense appetite. He denies any link between what he then termed the sensitive habits, and the argument is so closely linked with the habit-theory that it is doubtful whether it has any value when disassociated from the theory. Thus the non-existence of a link between so-called sensitive habits is deduced from the disparateness of the objects of the sensitive acts which, it was thought, caused these habits. According to Ockham's later theory,[43] the physiological conditions, credited with the attributes earlier ascribed to habits, were only indirectly brought about by the sensitive acts. Therefore

---

[42] Secunda conclusio quod quaecumque habitus partis sensitivae inclinans ad opera bona ex genere, sicut habitus partis sensitivae inclinans ad temperate comedendum, compatitur secum quodcumque vitium in voluntate, et contrarium virtuti voluntatis respectu illius objecti.—Rep. III. 11, MM.

[43] *Cf. Ante* p. 57.

the differences in the objects could not be expected to have as
important a bearing on the nature and interrelations of the residual
effects.[44]

Of greater interest to the moralist is the relation between the
moral virtues of the will and the intellectual habit of prudence, which
is the product of acts of assent to judgments of ethical import.
Ockham first views this relation from the side of prudence, and
states that it can exist without any virtuous act or habit in the will.
The proof is the fact that the will can refuse to conform to the dictates
of reason, which are identical with prudence viewed as acts; it can
do the exact opposite to that prescribed by prudence; or again, it can
suspend its activity and remain indifferent to reason's commands.
If acts of prudence, or right reason, can exist without moral virtues
in the will, then habits of prudence can also exist under the same
conditions.[45]

Viewing the relation between prudence and the moral virtues
of the will from the side of the latter now, Ockham acknowledges
greater dependence. In fact, neither virtuous acts nor virtuous habits
in the will can exist in the will without the prior existence of prudence, or right reason. It is essential to a virtuous act, continues Ockham, to be elicited in conformity with prudence or right reason.
Therefore there is a necessary connection between the virtues of the
will, on the one hand, and the acts and virtues, or habits, of prudence, on the other.[46]

---

[44] Loquendo de primis habitibus (*sensitivis*) sic dico quod non connectunt,
cuius ratio est quia habitus generatur ex actibus. Nunc autem potest aliquis
habere actum generativum unius habitum, licet non habet actum alterius
habitum, et frequenter exercere, sicut aliquis potest habere actum temperantiae
licet non fortitudinis.—Rep. III, 11, X.

[45] Et quantum ad istam dico quod prudentia potest esse sine virtutibus
moralibus, absque repugnantia. Quod probatur quia quicumque actus potest.
stare cum actu opposito virtuti potest generare habitum sine virtute. Sed actus
prudentiae est huiusmodi. Probatur quia voluntas potest velle oppositum
illius quod dictatum est a ratione. Unde si intellectus dictet quod omne dulce
est gustandum, voluntas potest discordare a ratione et potest velle oppositum;
potest etiam suspendere omnem actum. Sed actus quo voluntas vult oppositum
illius quod dictatum est a ratione est contra iudicium rationis, et per consequens
est actus viciosus. Igitur prudentia potest stare sine actu illius virtutis; et
similiter sicut arguitur de una virtute ita est arguendum de aliis.—Rep. III,
11, X.

[46] Secunda difficultas est de connexione virtutum moralium ad prudentiam.

The main problem regarding the connection of virtues, however, concerns the relation between virtues in the will itself. Here Ockham notes that according to the tradition established by Saints and philosophers these virtues are connected. But to determine the exact nature of this connection, the Venerabilis Inceptor describes two possible meanings of the term as accepted here. First, it could mean that virtues are formally. that is, intrinsically connected, so that the presence of one would entail the presence of the other or others. Secondly, it could mean that virtues are connected in such a manner that one disposes the subject, or inclines him, to acquire others; or at least the possession of one is not incompatible with the possession of any other.[47]

Taking the term in the first sense, Ockham denies any formal or intrinsic relation between virtues in the will. Thus, he would say the presence of one, either in a perfect state or imperfect state, does not necessarily entail the presence of any other, either in a perfect or imperfect state. The reason given stems from the fact that virtues are produced by acts and one virtuous act can be elicited without any thought of another. From this fact Ockham concludes that one virtue can be produced and augmented to a point of perfection independently of the presence or non-presence of any other.[48]

In the second acceptation, however, Ockham admits the possibility of a connection between virtues in the will. The impossibility of repugnance between these virtues can be deduced from their dependence on the dictates of reason, since the dictates are all linked

---

Et quantum ad istam dico quod virtus moralis perfecta non potest esse sine prudentia, et per consequens est necessaria connexio inter virtutes morales ad prudentiam. Quod probatur, quia de ratione virtutis et actus eius perfecte est quod eliciatur conformiter rationi rectae.—*Ibid.*

47 Tertia difficultas est de connexione virtutum moralium inter se. Et quantum ad istam dico quod secundum Sanctorum et philosophorum intentionem virtutes connectuntur. Sed earum connexio potest dupliciter intelligi: uno modo quod connectuntur seipsis formaliter, ita quod posita una virtute secundum gradum perfectum vel imperfectum, ponatur alia secundum perfectum vel imperfectum. Alio modo potest intelligi connexio dispositive, sive inclinative, sive privative.—Rep. III, 11, Y.

48 Primo dico quod non sunt connexae in gradu perfecto vel imperfecto. Cuius ratio est quia virtus generatur ex actibus determinatis. Nunc autem potest aliquis elicere actus unius virtutis, nihil cogitando de alia virtute. Igitur sic potest una sine alia generari et usque ad summum augmentari sine acquisitione alterius virtutis.—Rep. III, 11, Y.

to some general principles of moral conduct. Inasmuch as the dictates have a common source, the virtuous acts and habits of the will can also be described as having something in common. From this Ockham concludes that, at least, there is no incompatibility between the several moral virtues of the will. But is there any basis for a positive connection?[49]

Ockham sees the possibility of a causal connection between certain virtues of the will due to practical life situations. Thus the practice of one virtue, especially when it exists in a high degree of perfection, can dispose the subject to practice others when the circumstances call for them. Thus the Venerabilis Inceptor suggests the example of a person possessing virginal chastity in a perfect degree who is solicited to commit fornication and even threatened with violence in the case of resistance. This person would elicit acts of fortitude under these circumstances, even if he or she did not possess the virtue of fortitude at that moment. With respect to this initial act of fortitude the virtue of chastity, and more immediately the actual will to remain chaste, can be considered partial causes. Here then we have a case of one virtue causing another, at least indirectly. What is possible in one case, says Ockham, is possible in situations where any other virtue may be involved.[50]

---

[49] Secundo modo loquendo de connexione dico quod connectuntur dupliciter: uno modo quantum ad principia practica generalia communia omni virtuti, quae principia sunt praemissae principales inferentes conclusiones practicas, quibus habitus possunt in voluntate elici actus virtutis, et sine illis non.

Ex istis patet quod nulla virtus moralis repugnat alteri . . . Cuius ratio est quia omnis perfecta virtus moralis est conformis rationi rectae, quia aliter non esset virtus perfecta . . . Nunc autem contraria et formaliter repugnantia non sunt simul et semel conformia rectae rationi. Igitur istae virtutes non repugnant.—Rep. III, 11, Z.

[50] Alio modo connectuntur inclinative et dispositive, sic quod qui habet unam virtutem perfecte habet inclinationem et principium partiale efficiens respectu omnium virtutum. Exemplum: si enim aliquis habeat virginalem castitatem perfecte, et aliquis minetur sibi mortem vel vulnera, vel verbera, nisi fornicetur, iste habens perfecte castitatem virginalem, licet numquam habuit fortitudinem, quia numquam eliciebat actum fortitudinis, antequam tamen velit fornicari eligit suscipere vulnera, verbera et alia tormenta. Ista volitio vel electio est primus actus fortitudinis, et respectu istius actus est actus castitatis virginalis vel habitus causa efficiens immediata partialis. Et credo magis quod actus castitatis est causa alterius actus immediate, et habitus mediate . . . Et sicut est de fortitudine sic est de omni virtute morali.—Rep. III, 11, Z.

Under the heading of integration of virtues we have treated first of the relations between the residual effects of virtues of the will on the passions. Ockham's final thinking on this question is a matter of conjecture, though it can be said that in the period when he held the possibility of habits in the sense appetite he admitted, of no connection between these habits. Secondly, we studied the relations between prudence and the virtues of the will. This was seen to be a one-sided relation, in the sense that while prudence could subsist without these virtues, they themselves required the prior existence of prudence. Thirdly, the connection between the virtues of the will was examined. This was found to be not a necessary intrinsic relation, whereby the existence of one automatically produced any other, but a contingent relation, arising out of the conditions of practical moral conduct. One virtue, at least in its perfect state, could in certain circumstances be a partial cause of other virtues, at least, indirectly.

A review of this chapter will recall the main thought of each of the six sections. The first section showed that according to Ockham the subjective basis of moral virtue was the will, and more particularly that attribute of the will whereby it has power and dominion over its acts and those of the potencies of man.

In the second section Ockham's views on the objective norm or norms of morality were examined. These consisted in the precepts of the divine will in their particular applications to each person.

In the third the different elements of a complete virtuous act were listed and described. These elements were all qualified as objects of the virtuous act by Ockham because by that he meant to underscore the fact that none of them could be changed without affecting the specific nature and numeric unity of the act. They included the dictates of right reason, the end of the act, the sensitive passions, or acts, and physical actions which have specific settings in time and space.

The fourth discussed the question of the moral indifference of the sense passions, and showed how some passions had to be aroused and others quelled by the virtues of the will. It further explained how one and the same virtue could have reference to opposing passions on the sense level.

The fifth dealt with the more permanent effects caused by the virtues of the will on the sensitive and physiological level. Ockham consistently maintained that such residual effects were observable as a result of the practice of virtue. But he reversed his earlier stand on the point of habit in this connection, and later contended that these residual effects were simply physiological conditions. In any case, he maintained that these were not a prerequisite for real virtue; and on the other hand, these effects, once produced on the lower level, could subsist after the virtue or virtues of the will had disappeared.

The sixth and last division of this last chapter treated the question of the relations between the effect of one virtue and that of another; the relations between the virtues of the will and the acts and habits of prudence; and finally, the relations between the virtues of the will itself.

V. Summary and Conclusion

In summing up our findings with regard to habit in Ockham's works, the first point to be emphasized is that he defines habit in function of certain definite facts of observation or experience. It is an acquired ability through repetition of acts to do things in a manner or with a degree of perfection unknown before. Theorizing upon these data, Ockham establishes a causal relationship between acts which produce habit and habit itself on the one hand, and habit and the acts resulting from it, on the other. The basis for differentiating between habits was sought in the specific differences between acts. Thus, acts which were specifically alike but only numerically diverse could contribute to the formation of one habit. The scope of a habit was considered as broad as that of the acts which produced it. Thus, to a comprehensive act encompassing many individual, simple acts could correspond an equally comprehensive habit.

Taking up the study of habit more in detail, we first examined its role in the cognitive processes. In these processes Ockham distinguished between intuitive cognition and abstractive, the former relating to existential knowledge and the latter to non-existential. All habit-formation was denied in the former, but it was posited in the latter. To account for retention and recall by the intellect of individual past experience, Ockham postulated initial reflexive acts by which these subjective experiences were cognized as such and which could produce habits. These habits performed the basic functions of memory. Forgetting was explained as the process of deterioration of such habits through the action, especially, of physiological causes. No habit was recognized in the cognition of the external senses. In the imagination, however, it served to explain this faculty's ability to revive past experiences in the absence of the object which contributed to the initial experience.

In the realm of conative experiences there are in Ockham's system three levels of activity which permit of habit-formation: the volitive, the sensitive and the physical. With regard to the first he consistently maintained the possibility of habit, though he was critical of the arguments usually adduced to establish this point. On the sensitive level his final stand was against habit. Those facts of experience which earlier lead him to postulate it on this level can be equally well explained, he contended, on the basis of physiological conditions. On the physical level Ockham accounted for skills on the basis of habit.

The moral aspects of the habit-theory have traditionally been viewed as its most important features. In examining Ockham's exposition of this phase of habit we remarked that for him the will was the subjective basis of morality and the will of God the objective norm of virtuous behaviour. Cast in the role of objects of virtuous acts are the dictates of right reason, the end of the act, the sensitive passions, and physical actions involving time and place. The influence of virtuous habits of the will on the lower passions was studied in some detail. It was seen how they derived their morality from the habits and acts of the will. Then the question of residual effects on the sensitive level as results of the influence of the virtues of the will was brought up. And Ockham's answer was that no habit need be postulated on the sensitive level. Discussing the relations of the moral habits with the intellectual habit of prudence, it was noted that it can exist without them, whereas they cannot exist without it. Between the virtues of the will, finally, there is some connection, but this is not an internal or intrinsic relationship. It can be said to have an external basis due to the fact that all moral behaviour is linked with a definite set of moral principles. Furthermore, in actual life-situations the practice of one virtue can entail the practice of any other virtue according to the circumstances. With this summary in mind it may be permitted to draw a few general conclusions. which may help to appreciate Ockham's contribution to the theory of habit.

Habit in Ockham's system is linked with certain definite data of experience, but it is distinct from these. It is of a different order of reality, because it is a theoretical explanation of these data. Any attempt to contain it within the confines of observable neural patterns is doomed to failure from the outset. Yet, this attempt was made by the early experimentalists in psychology. Today it is recognized by all that "it is futile to attempt to continue a physiological theory of learning."[1]

---

[1] K. Dunlap, Habits, *Their Making and Unmaking*, p. 83.

Still greater damage was done to the traditional habit-theory, as crystallized in Ockham's writings, by those who accepted it while rejecting the more basic factors of Scholastic Psychology, namely the faculties and the substantial form. It was assumed that all learning could be reduced to habit-formation without postulating these basic factors. In other words, it was supposed that human intelligent behaviour could be explained without positing an intelligence or a soul.

At the beginning this approach seemed valid to many. It ushered in the era of psychological tests and measurements. But as the exact nature of learning became increasingly clearer and the integrative processes of the mind were once more recognized, serious doubts began to arise concerning it. Finally this conception of habit exploded completely.[2] Then there remained only questions and no answers in the minds of certain modern psychologists. They asked themselves: how could the repetition of acts explain the apparent progressive, creative aspects of the learning process? How could habit account for the fact that in many learning situations the *learned* response surpassed the *learning* response? Can one explain on the basis of habit-formation how the playing of a beautiful melody is learned by the continuous repetition of certain chords and scales? Habit in its traditional formulation, they concluded, was tried and found wanting.

Our conclusion is that habit had been cast in a role for which it was not made. Never had Medieval philosophers attempted to explain all learning on the basis of habit-formation. At best, habit was considered an auxiliary power. May we end with this pointed remark: until a place is once more found in modern systems for the factors which formed the backbone of the classical theories of learning, that is, the intelligence, the will, and the soul, etc. the habit-theory will, we feel, continue to be the stumbling-block it has become for so many.

---

[2] K. Dunlap, *op. cit.* p. 35.

BIBLIOGRAPHY

Aristotle, *The Basic Works of,* New York: R. McKeon, 1941.

——, *Opera Omnia.* Paris: Firmin-Didot et Soc. 5 Vols. 1927.

——, ——, Berlin: I. Bekker, 1831-1870.

Averroes, *Aristotelis Libri Omnes cum Averrois Commentariis,* Venice, Apud Iuntas, 1550, 13 Vols.

Boehner, P., "The Notitia Intuitiva of Non-existents according to Ockham," *Traditio,* I, (1943), 223-275.

——, "The Text Tradition of Ockham's Ordinatio," *The New Scholasticism,* XVI (1942), 203-241.

——, *The Tractatus de Successivis, attributed to Ockham,* Franciscan Institute Publications, No. 1. St. Bonaventure, N.Y., 1944, 122 pp.

Bourke, V. "Habitus in St. Thomas as a Metaphysical Perfectant of Potency," Unpublished Doctoral Dissertation, The University of Toronto, 1939.

Day, S., *Intuitive Cognition: A Key to the Significance of the Later Scholastics,* Franc. Instit. Publ. No. 4. St. Bonaventure, N.Y., 1947, 217 pp.

Dunlap, K., *Habits, Their Making and Unmaking.* New York: Liveright Publishing Company, 1932, 326 pp.

Hochstetter, E., *Studien zur Metaphysik und Erkenntnislehre Wilhelms von Ockham,* Berlin, Leipzig: Walter de Gruyter and Co., 1927, 179 pp.

Ockham, William, *Expositio Aurea Super Artem Veterem,* Bologna: Marcus de Benevento, 1496.

——, *Expositio Super Octo Libros Physicorum.* (Prologue, G. Mohan, ed. *Franciscan Studies,* V (1945) p. 235-246.)

——, *Ordinatio* (Commentarius in 1um Librum Sententiarum), Lyons, 1495.

——, ——, (Quaestio 1a Prologi, P. Boehner, ed. Paderborn: Schoeningh, 1940).

——, ——, (Quaestio 8a Dist. 2ae, P. Boehner, ed. *The New* Scholasticism, XVI (1942), p. 224-241.

——, *Quaestiones Variae* (Rep. III, 12-15), Lyons, 1495.

——, *Quodlibeta VII,* Ms. Vat. lat. 3075.

——, ——, Strassbourg, 1491; Paris, 1487.

——, *Reportatio* (Quaestiones in 2um, 3um, 4um, Libros Sententiarum) Mss. Oxford, Balliol, Coll. 299; Firenze, Bibl. Naz. A. 3. 801; Paris, Bibl. Mazar. 893, XIV cent.

——, ——, Lyons, 1495.

——, *Summa Totius Logicae,* Venice, 1508.

——, *Summulae in Libros Physicorum,* Venice, 1506.

Rooney, M. A., "A Comparison of the Notions of Habitus in the Philosophy of St. Thomas and Godfrey of Fontaines," Unpublished Doctoral Dissertation, Universite de Montreal, 1949.

Scotus, John Duns, *Opera Omnia,* Paris, Vives, 1891-1895, 26 Vols. Thomas of Aquin, St., *Opera Omnia,* Parmae, 1858.

——, *Summa Theologica,* Ottawa, 1941.

INDEX

Abstraction, process of, 24, 31ff

Abstractive cognition, 21, 22-29, 45ff

Acts, basis of distinction of habits, 11ff; causes of habits, 7ff; effects of habits, 8ff; end of, 90

Act-passions, *see* Passions, primary

Appetite, sense level, 49f; intellective, 64ff

Appetitive experiences, 49-80

Aristotle, xii, xiii-xiv, 3, 5, 6, 19, 20, 25, 41, 43, 47, 52, 53, 59, 75, 80, 94

Assent, 89, 99.

Averroes, xiv, 3

Boehner, P., xviii, 20, n.5; 22, n.12: 30, n.34; 55, n.20

Bourke, V., xii

Categories, number of, 2-3

Cognitive processes, 18-49

Complex Cognition, 12, 15, 30, 37, 38

Conative experiences, 49-80

Concepts, formed from singular, 13, 31ff

Connection of virtues, 16, 98-104

Connotative terms, 3, 7, n.18

Continence, 95f.

Criterion of habit, 1ff

Definition of habit, 1ff, 78

Deterioration of habit, 41f, 47

Differentiation of habits, 11-13

Dispositions, related to habit, , 41ff, 56ff

Distinctions, real and grammatical, 52

·Duns Scotus, *see* Scotus

Effects of habit, 8-11

Emotions, *see* Passions

End of acts, 90

Essence and existence, 19, 23, 50

Existence of habit, 1ff

Faculties, distinction of, 7, n.18; 10, 50; as subjects of habit, 9

Faith, habit of, 16

Falsity, in judgments, 3

Fear, 65, 94

Fictum, 30, *see also* note 35

Forgetting, 39-42, 47

Formation of habits, 5-8

Fortitude, 94, 101

Free will, *see* Liberty

Genus, as a concept, 30ff

God, first cause of habit-formation, 39; 59f, 81f

Godfrey of Fontaines, xii, xvi

Habit, cause of, 5ff; cognitive, 18-49 cognitive on the sense level, 42-49; cognitive on the intellective level, 18-42; conative, 49-76; conative on the sense level, 49-64; conative on the intellective or volitive level, 64-76; criterion of, 1ff; definition of, 1ff, 78; differentiation of, 11-13; effects of, 8-11; formation of, 5-8; inborn or acquired, ·5ff; integration of, 13-17, moral, 80-104

Hunger, as a passion, 55

Hochstetter, E., 22, n.12; 26, n.25

Imagination, *see* Phantasm

Imperfect intuitive cognition, 34ff

Inclination, sensitive, 62-64, 71-76; volitive, 69-71

Incomplex cognition, 11f, 15, 18, 23, 27

Indifference of passions, 91

Indifferent moral acts, 83f

Integration of habits, 13-17; in concepts, 32ff; in moral principles, 98-102

Intellect, as a faculty, 7, n.18; 9

Intellective cognition, habits in, 18-42; object of, 23

www.ingramcontent.com/pod-product-compliance
Lightning Source LLC
Chambersburg PA
CBHW071820090426
42737CB00012B/2144